SEW and PLAY
HANDMADE GAMES FOR KIDS

FARAH WOLFE

Martingale
Create with Confidence

Sew and Play: Handmade Games for Kids
© 2014 by Farah Wolfe

Martingale®
19021 120th Ave. NE, Ste. 102
Bothell, WA 98011-9511 USA
ShopMartingale.com

Printed in China
19 18 17 16 15 14   8 7 6 5 4 3 2 1

Library of Congress Cataloging-in-Publication Data
is available upon request.

ISBN: 978-1-60468-454-4

MISSION STATEMENT

Dedicated to providing quality products
and service to inspire creativity.

CREDITS

PUBLISHER AND CHIEF VISIONARY OFFICER:
Jennifer Erbe Keltner

EDITOR IN CHIEF: Mary V. Green

DESIGN DIRECTOR: Paula Schlosser

MANAGING EDITOR: Karen Costello Soltys

ACQUISITIONS EDITOR: Karen M. Burns

TECHNICAL EDITOR: Ellen Pahl

COPY EDITOR: Tiffany Mottet

PRODUCTION MANAGER: Regina Girard

COVER AND INTERIOR DESIGNER: Adrienne Smitke

PHOTOGRAPHER: Brent Kane

ILLUSTRATOR: Christine Erikson

Special thanks to Sabrina and Eric Howell of
Seattle, Washington, for generously allowing us to
photograph in their home. Also thanks to Maddie,
Otis, Hailey, and Luke for being such cute and
enthusiastic models.

For my Grandmother, Frances,
who played with us for hours

Contents

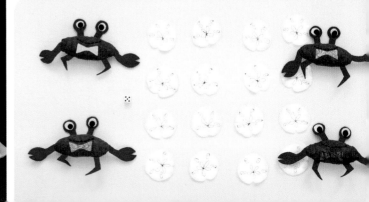

Introduction

Children are playful creatures. They have a natural inclination to learn, explore, and manipulate their environment. Their imaginations are limitless; their senses are vibrant and full of life. Whether you are a parent, an aunt or uncle, a grandparent, an educator, or a therapist, *Sew and Play* offers you the opportunity to nurture this beautiful and delightful journey through sewing.

The 11 projects in *Sew and Play* will allow you to create games that children of all ages can enjoy. Follow the simple sewing instructions, copy the game sheet, and you will have a game that children will ask to play again and again. The games in this book are washable, lightweight, friendly to the senses, and oh-so lovable. They are easy to construct, do not require perfection, and can be made by novice crafters and sewists. These games require no batteries, they are gender neutral, and each game offers playing opportunities for two age groups: toddlers/preschoolers and school-aged kids. These games are unique and engaging, and they will outlast many store-bought toys. Best of all, you will enjoy making them.

If you *engage* kids, they will play. So let's begin!

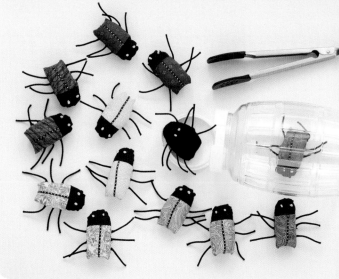

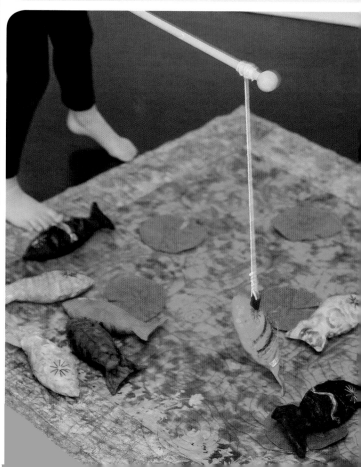

Tidbits, Tools, and Techniques

Before embarking on any of the projects in this book, take the time to read the tidbits in this section. They will provide some useful information, as well as offer opportunities to spark your creativity. Then check out "Tools and Techniques" (page 13) to make sure you have on hand all that you need to be successful.

how this book is organized

The games are arranged according to the skill level required for their construction—the first projects being the easiest and the final projects requiring a bit more time and skill. A crafter with intermediate sewing skills can readily make all of the projects. Each project includes a materials list and complete instructions for assembly and sewing, as well as rules for playing.

At times you'll be referred to the techniques chapter for additional instructions that apply to multiple projects, such as applying fusible web or how to maneuver a specific hand stitch. Each project also offers tips and a variety of suggestions for packaging and storing the game, often including a drawstring bag. You'll frequently encounter references to specific sections in "Game Accessories" (starting on page 103) for more detailed instructions, since many of the projects include similar suggestions for packaging. This reduces redundancy and allows more space for games. So continue on and enjoy your journey sewing these unique and fun-filled creations!

imagination = personality, not perfection

The less realistic your creatures, the more kids will use their imaginations to fill in the gaps. Unique and imperfect characters and game pieces are naturally more inviting to children. Factory produced, perfectly identical toys lack this warmth of character. The traits that we end up loving in our toys come from the details that make them unique. Do you think a child will politely decline to play your game because your seams are not perfect? Probably not. So let go, breathe out, and keep these projects fun.

about the game sheets

Each project, when completed, will become a dynamic game for children to play. Each has playing options for various developmental stages, which means these games will grow with the child. The game and play suggestions for toddlers and preschoolers are designed as "Mom/Dad and me" activities. At this age, children benefit from the guidance of an adult. These are play-based activities that nurture learning and lay the foundation for important life skills. The games for school-aged children also encourage many important skills, but will require less direction from an adult—although all adults are welcome to play!

The game sheets in this book are ready-to-use written instructions on how to play. Your only task is to reproduce or duplicate this game sheet. Here are a few ways to do that.

* **Photocopy.** Take your book to a copy center. Use the self-service option, or have an employee copy the Game Sheet page for a small fee.

* **Scan.** Scan the game sheet page into your computer and print it out at home. You can use decorative stationary, colored card stock, printable fabric sheets that can be incorporated into the game storage bag, or use just plain white paper. They all work.

* **Type and print.** If you don't have a scanner, type out the game sheet information on your own and print it out. You'll need to use this method if you change the theme of the game (refer to "Alternate Themes," page 12, for details).

* **Handwrite.** For those who prefer to not involve modern technology, you can hand print the game sheet onto paper, or directly onto fabric using a fine-point permanent marker. This is a great way to personalize your games.

* **Laminate.** For any of the methods above, you have the option of laminating your game sheets for longer life. Many copy centers provide this service. You can also purchase laminated sheets to use yourself or purchase clear contact paper, available at most large grocery or discount stores. Just sandwich the game sheet between two pieces of contact paper, sticky sides together. Apply one side at a time, smooth out, and then trim the edges, leaving a ½"-wide border of contact paper to keep it together.

simplifying

Some of these projects have foundations (such as play mats) that essentially involve constructing a small quilt with or without a binding. For novice crafters or those wishing to finish a game quickly, you can substitute some easier variations that require less skill, time, and materials. Refer to "Foundations" on page 110 if you want to start small or save time. If you're an experienced quilter, you will likely find the binding and piecing techniques I use to be full of shortcuts. Feel free to finish the quilt foundation using techniques you're familiar

with. Keep in mind, however, the little quilt judges will probably be too busy playing to care about the details.

Another way to simplify is to use felt. I like to think of felt as easy way out. It's possible for many of these projects to be made completely of felt. Since felt doesn't fray and has no right or wrong side, you won't have to turn pieces right side out, or hand stitch any openings closed. Simply use the patterns to trace and cut the felt, sew the pieces together using a ¼" seam allowance, stuff with fiberfill if required (as in the fish and bugs), and then topstitch the opening closed with your sewing machine. While these may not have the same crafted appearance, they will play the same. I always recommend using premium felt, purchased off the bolt. It's much more durable than the thinner craft felt sheets.

fabric and construction

Throughout this book, I suggest using cotton fabric, but by no means are you limited to cotton. I chose it because it's a natural fiber, which automatically makes it friendly for me. Cotton washes well, holds up to excessive use, comes in an infinite variety of colors and patterns, doesn't fray beyond reason, stretches very little, and it is easy to sew. You're welcome to use any other fabrics, just keep in mind the characteristics mentioned above. Remember, durability is important. These games are meant to be played with, which may entail being stepped on, kicked, chewed, thrown, stuffed in unusual places, and ultimately washed and abused all over again (another thing to consider when you scrutinize your work for perfection, right?).

On a few projects, I suggest vinyl, available at most fabric stores. It's strong, wipes clean, doesn't wrinkle or fray, and is more conducive to outdoor play. Vinyl also requires less skill and labor. There are greener and more economical alternatives, such as heavyweight premium felt or recycled leather. You could also apply heavyweight single-sided fusible stabilizer to a variety of cotton fabrics to create a stiff, nearly wrinkle-free product. (For further instructions, refer to "Fusible Stabilizer" on page 16. If you use this, I suggest using a fray preventative on the edges.) The fusing technique could easily be used to replace the vinyl horses in "Horse Race" on page 46.

go green: making eco-friendly games

The projects in this book are not only fun, they're a much greener alternative to bulky, plastic, battery-operated toys that litter the toy-store shelves. Plastic toys that entertain a child for six months will likely take more than a thousand years to biodegrade in our growing landfills. The games in this book are designed to grow with the child, and their properties are much gentler on the earth. If you're the environmentally conscious sort, here are a few ways to make these games even more eco friendly.

* **Buy second hand.** I love to peruse garage sales and secondhand shops. You never know what unique gem you may find! Buying an item that has been gently used is an easy and effective way to recycle and reduce our carbon footprint. Used clothing, window treatments, and bedding can offer a great selection of fabrics. Additionally, you can find some unique containers for packaging your games.

* **Repurpose.** Search the back of your closets, your attic, and under your bed. Unused household items can provide some wonderful and unlikely contributions to these projects. Baskets, bags, boxes, purses, tins, and other containers can be painted, decoupaged, or embellished with fabric scraps to create some great storage containers for games.

* **Select natural fabrics and fibers.** When shopping for fiberfill stuffing, choose more natural fibers. There are pros and cons to them all. Do some research to decide what works best for your lifestyle and budget. Alternatives to polyester include cotton, wool, bamboo, kapok, hemp, and even corn fiber. Many polyester fiberfill products are now made from recycled material—just check the label. For projects that use vinyl, refer to "Using Double-Sided Fusible Stabilizer" on page 16 for instructions on substituting fabric for vinyl. Use natural materials for adding weight to projects. Get creative. Wrap a small, smooth river stone in some batting and nestle it into your game piece instead of plastic pellets. (Read "Safety Considerations" below.)

The sky is the limit. Think outside of the box (or the big-box store!) and teach our next generation how recycling can transform into fun while helping the planet at the same time.

safety considerations

Anyone who has watched a baby for more than five seconds knows that babies put pretty much *everything* they encounter into their mouths for further exploration. When making these games, I encourage adding sensory elements (bells, crinkly cellophane, etc.) to several of them. These are "small parts" and, therefore, it is extremely important that you understand the safety concerns before you start construction of these projects. Many fun elements, such as buttons and bells, are choking hazards to the three-and-under crowd. Long cords can get unintentionally wrapped around little body parts.

Don't use pellets, or any object smaller than 1¾", in items for children under three years old. In *Sew and Play*, similar to commercial infant toys, these items are sewn inside of the characters, not loose for a child to encounter. Use your discretion.

Children this young should be supervised at all times with these games. The playing options for younger players all require the guidance of an adult. Of course, constant supervision isn't always the reality. So, if you're going to add these elements, here are a few tips to help reduce any risks.

* **Sew 'em up good!** If a toddler is on the list of players, and you have added sensory elements to these game pieces (bells, beads, cellophane, etc.), sew these game pieces using the full ½" seam allowance that is provided in the patterns to decrease the risk of fabric fraying, which could lead to these sensory elements falling out. (For the snakes in "Snake Pit," you will need to add additional seam allowance to the pattern on page 66.) In addition, stitching twice, adding a zigzag stitch next to the seam line, and fray preventative to the cut (raw) edge will offer additional hole prevention. For added security, make a separate fabric tube to hold pellets for weighting objects. (Refer to "Making the Boats," step 6, in "Treasure Island" on page 96.)

* **Secure buttons.** Use a double-threaded needle and stitch back and forth until your needle and thread no longer fit through the holes of the button. Then knot the tail multiple times before trimming the thread. Buttons secured this way are virtually indestructible.

* **Cords are for big kids.** Toddlers can easily become tangled in cords and they don't have the skills to untangle themselves. Keep any cords longer than 6" out of the reach of small children. None of the playing options for these little ones require cords.

* **Inspect, inspect, inspect.** Check the games frequently for any developing holes or tears and fix or replace them immediately.

Be thoughtful while sewing, take the time to consider these points, and make safety a top priority.

alternate themes

These games are great springboards for alternative themes. They offer many opportunities for you to personalize them to match the interests of the children who will be playing. You could easily turn "Monster Ball" into "Space Ball" by making planets instead of monsters, and choosing a dark-blue starry fabric for the background. "Gone Fishin'" could become "Flower Pickin'" or "Veggie Pickin'" by making stuffed flowers or veggies instead of fish, and then making the pond into a garden patch. "Horse Race" could become "Turtle Race," or even "Race Cars." "Bug Hunt" could be "Butterfly Hunt," or "Dinosaur Hunt" with a caterpillar or a dinosaur egg to replace the spider. The possibilities for creativity are limitless.

I CAN'T DRAW!

Making a game with your own theme can be easy and fun. You don't have to be a skilled illustrator or even an amateur artist to make your own patterns. Simplicity is the key. Sources of inspiration are all around you. Just start flipping through basic coloring books, observe cartoon images in storybooks and on children's clothing and you will begin to find a wealth of easy-to-duplicate images that could make great patterns. You can also use photographs, tracing only the basic parts until you are satisfied with the image. The Internet offers many options if you search for silhouettes, line drawings, cartoons, and black-and-white images. Just remember to respect copyrights and make any images you find your own by modifying or redrawing them. Your priceless reward will be experiencing the laughter and joy of children playing your games.

tools and techniques

This section offers you a reference for the tools and techniques used throughout this book. From fusing to French knots, it will be your guide when you need it.

Free-Motion Stitching

Many of these projects suggest using free-motion stitching on your sewing machine. Free-motion sewing or quilting not only saves time, but also allows you to stitch curves, swirls, and a wide array of designs without bunching up your fabric or having to stop and pivot the fabric constantly.

In order to sew in this manner, you'll need to swap the regular presser foot with a darning foot. Most sewing machines come with one. You'll use it as you would any presser foot, making sure to bring the lever down before sewing. The darning foot allows you to essentially freehand draw with your stitching. You'll be moving the fabric, while the machine does the stitching. Consult your sewing-machine owner's manual for specific details on using your darning foot. You may need to lower the feed dogs and shorten the stitch length. This is a great, creative way to use your machine. Practice is all you need.

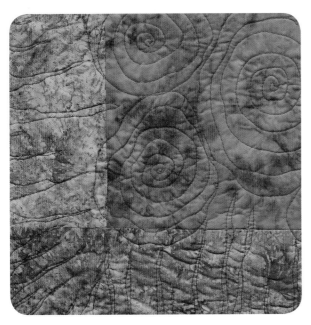

Free-motion designs on the pond mat of "Gone Fishin'" (page 84).

Water - waves

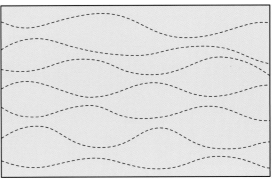

Swirls - whimsical

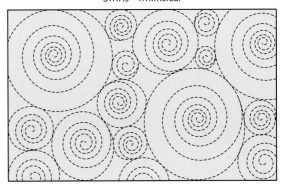

Continuous lines

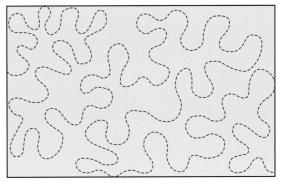

Flowers

Fusible Web

Fusible web is a fun and easy-to-use iron-on adhesive. It comes in paper-like sheets or rolls, and can be applied to the wrong side of fabric to create a glue that is activated by heat from an iron. Remember those fuzzy iron-on letters you could buy to put on T-shirts? Well, this product can transform any fabric into an "iron-on." Its uses are vast, and the variety of products and manufacturers are just as plentiful. Many of the details in these projects have been applied using fusible web.

When shopping for fusible web, you'll notice there are sewable products and non-sewable products. If you plan to add some decorative stitching for detail, then choose the sewable kind. It's lightweight and easy to sew through, and since the fabric has been fused, it makes decorative appliqué or topstitching a breeze. Your fabric will not shift and the needle glides easily through it. I recommend adding some stitching to secure the fabric and guarantee that it stays on for the long run. This is especially important for games that will see lots of use!

If you're short on time and want to "iron and run," then the non-sewable or "No-Sew" variety offers a more permanent bond. Keep in mind that it can't be sewn later if you change your mind. The adhesive will gum up your needle and shred your thread, making it tough to sew through and hard on your sewing machine.

Fusible products can be bought in sheets, by the roll, or measured off the bolt. Any of these can work for the projects in this book, but some may be more convenient to work with than others. (The roll offers more width and length; you may need to piece the smaller sheets together for some projects.) Buying a roll or buying by the yard is cheaper in the long run if you're going to be using it often. Each project will specify the amount you need.

Instructions for using fusible web vary from one brand to another. Some require steam, and some require a dry iron. The timing on each product is slightly different. So, throughout the book where fusible web is used, I defer to manufacturer's instructions. That said, there are some basic instructions for using fusible products.

1. Trace the pattern onto the paper side of the fusible web. This can usually be done directly from the book pages.

2. Cut around the traced lines, leaving at least ¼" on all sides.

3. Place the fusible shape adhesive side (the bumpy side) down on the wrong side of the fabric. Use an iron to fuse the shape to the fabric, following the manufacturer's instructions.

4. Allow the adhesive to cool completely, and then cut out the shape exactly on the traced lines.

Wrong side of appliqué fabric

Paper side of fusible web

5. Peel off the paper backing. Under the paper backing you'll see that the fabric is coated with something shiny or with a matte finish (depending on the product). This is the fusible web, the adhesive. If some of the adhesive is still sticking to the paper as you remove it, gently lay the paper back over the fabric, and use the iron again. After it's cool, try removing the paper. You want all of the fusible web to be adhered to the fabric so the paper comes off cleanly.

6. Position the appliqué fabric right side up onto the right side of the background fabric where you'll be permanently affixing it. Using your iron, fuse it in place as directed. Right side up means the side with the adhesive will be in direct contact with the background fabric.

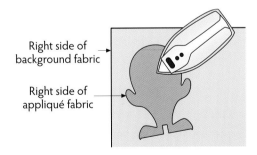

Right side of background fabric

Right side of appliqué fabric

7. Let the fabric cool completely, and then check all edges to make sure they have completely fused to the background. If not, follow the manufacturer's instructions to reapply the iron. Again, wait until the fabric has cooled.

The glue is not permanent or "dry" until it has cooled completely.

On occasion, you may be directed to apply the fusible web to the fabric before cutting the shapes. This is done for the windows on the boats in "Treasure Island" (page 92) and for the eyes on the monsters in "Monster Ball" (page 31). Cut the fusible web slightly smaller than the fabric. With the fabric wrong side up, place the fusible web on top of the fabric, paper side up and iron as directed. Wait for the fabric to cool completely. At this point, you can cut the pieces as instructed in the project. With this method, you can also draw the pattern onto the fused fabric, or draw the reverse of the pattern onto the paper side. Cut out the shape, peel off the paper backing, and fuse the shape to the background.

TIPS FOR FUSING FABRIC

* *Prewash all fabric. Any coatings, or dyes left in the fabric will inhibit the adhesive from reaching its full fusible potential. Don't use fabric softener or dryer sheets.*

* *Some fabrics are more fuse-friendly than others. Remember you'll be pressing this fabric with an iron, so synthetic material that has a tendency to melt at high temperatures probably won't be the best choice.*

* *A Teflon sheet works great for protecting your iron if you do a lot of projects with fusible web. Any leftover paper backing can also be used as a convenient protective barrier.*

* *Batiks are beautiful, but will likely need to be stitched after fusing. Something in the resists and dyes used in the batik process limits the ability of the adhesive to fully bond to the fabric.*

Fusible Stabilizer

Similar to fusible web, fusible stabilizer comes in various levels of firmness, just as traditional stabilizer does. Fusible stabilizer is used for everything from garments and decorative bowls to these delightful children's games. The stabilizer becomes part of the item, making it strong and durable. It's typically found on the bolt and can be measured and cut to your preference. The stabilizer can be single sided or double sided, which means that the fusible adhesive is on either one or both sides. The projects in this book specify which type you'll need.

USING SINGLE-SIDED FUSIBLE STABILIZER

Single-sided fusible stabilizer only has adhesive on one side. Use an iron to fuse the wrong side of the fabric to the adhesive side of the stabilizer. In this case, place the stabilizer adhesive side up and place the fabric right side up on top. Make sure no stabilizer is exposed, and then iron as directed. Using a Teflon sheet will protect your iron from adhesive.

USING DOUBLE-SIDED FUSIBLE STABILIZER

This product has adhesive on both sides. Sandwich the fusible stabilizer between two layers of fabric, and then iron as directed (typically on both sides). The right sides of the fabric should both be facing out, with the wrong sides against the stabilizer. (This technique could be used in "Horse Race" on page 46 in place of the vinyl.)

Hand Stitches

I used hand sewing to finish several of the projects in this book and to add embellishment details. Here are the details of the stitches that I used.

LADDER STITCH

Use the ladder stitch to hand sew a stuffed item closed. With practice, it's quite easy. If you've never tried it before, try sewing and stuffing some scraps, and then sew the opening closed with the ladder stitch. It's called a ladder stitch because of the back-and-forth pattern the thread makes as you sew.

1. Double thread your needle and knot the end securely.

2. Using the fold in the seam as a guide, insert the needle at the beginning of the opening. Bring it from the inside out through the folded crease to hide the knot on the interior.

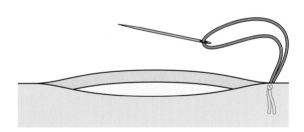

3. Keep the crease defined, holding the seam together the way you plan to sew it. Slip the needle through the opposite side, sliding it through the fabric and under the fold 1/16" away. (Use very close stitches to make the closure secure.)

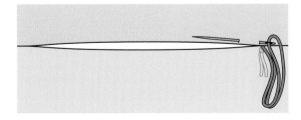

4. Bring the needle back to the first side, once again hiding the needle and thread in the fold, moving along 1/16" and then back across to the other side. This is where you'll start to see the ladder pattern you are creating. Continue stitching, pulling the stitches snug as you sew. They should be well concealed when you do so, and the opening should close smoothly, without puckers.

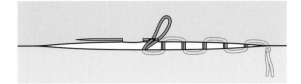

5. Continue stitching until the opening is completely closed. Take two or three stitches in the same place to secure the thread. Knot the thread a few times, insert the needle into the batting or stuffing to bury the knot, and bring it out about ½" away. Trim the thread next to the fabric.

FRENCH KNOT

The French knot is an embroidery stitch that I use as a decorative element. It's safe around teething babies and toddlers, and when using double-threaded embroidery floss, it can be as bold as a bead. If you've never done this stitch before, practice on scrap fabric before stitching on your project.

1. Double thread your embroidery needle with all six strands of embroidery floss and knot the end securely. You'll be working with a total of 12 strands to create a nice, bold knot.

2. Bring the needle up through the wrong side of the fabric, pulling it to the knot. This will hide the knot on the wrong side, or what will be the inside of your project.

3. At the base of your thread, where it comes out of the fabric, wrap the thread around the end of your needle three to four times. (I did four wraps for the bug and snake eyes.)

4. Hold the thread tightly a few inches from the wrapped base with your non-sewing hand. Insert the needle directly next to where you came up through the fabric. Push the needle down, keeping hold of the thread as you pull the needle through the fabric. When your thread is almost completely through the fabric, and just a small loop remains, let go of the thread. The French knot should form as you pull the rest of the thread tight. Make a knot on the wrong side of the fabric to secure.

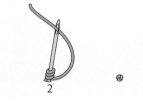

French Knot

This is one of the most basic hand-embroidery stitches, and it's super easy.

1. Double thread your needle with all six strands of embroidery floss and knot the end securely.

2. Bring the needle up through the wrong side of the fabric, pulling it to the knot. This will hide the knot on the wrong side, or what will be the inside of your project.

3. Following the line you are stitching on, push the needle back through the right side of the fabric about ⅛" from your starting point. Pull this stitch tight.

4. Bring the needle back up through the wrong side of the fabric, just a hair, or ¹⁄₁₆" from where your last stitch ended. Pull this stitch up, and then insert the needle back through the right side of the fabric about ⅛" from this point to create a nice embroidered line.

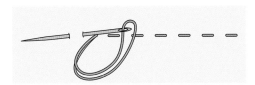

Running stitch

5. As you get comfortable with this stitch, try weaving your needle in, and out of the top of the fabric in this same fashion in order to complete two or three stitches at a time. Pull the thread taught before starting your next series of weaves.

6. When you reach the end of the line to be stitched, push the needle back through to the wrong side of the fabric, and knot the ends securely.

parts from parachute cord

Parachute cord makes wonderful appendages for all kinds of creatures, from snake tongues to bug legs. You just need to seal the ends to keep them from fraying. This is incredibly easy and makes them look like real tongues or cute little bug feet.

1. Clear off a stable surface, preferably near a sink (just in case) and lay down a sheet of scrap cardboard to protect the work surface.

2. Light a candle, a safe distance from the cardboard, or use a lighter. One at a time, hold the tip of the parachute cord in the flame for approximately five seconds (time may vary depending on the gauge of the cord). For short pieces, you may want to use pliers to hold the cord in the flame. The end will melt into a little ball. Some candles may leave a bit of soot that will show up on light-colored cord, such as pink. Use a lighter for a clean, clear seal.

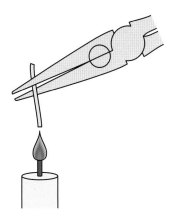

3. Set the cord on the cardboard to cool and continue with the rest of the pieces. You only need to seal one end for legs or tongues, but I usually do both ends for extra fray prevention.

Capture the Tag

Capture the Tag is a fantastic game for getting kids to be active; there's no sitting down for this one! Easy to sew and endless fun to play, Capture the Tag requires movement, body awareness, and good hand-eye coordination for a fun new dynamic to the classic games of chase and team tag. Younger kids will be entertained by the colors and amazed by the magical properties of Velcro. Get out your scraps for this project; you can complete it over an afternoon cup of coffee.

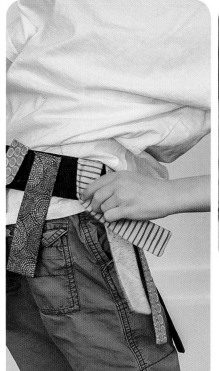

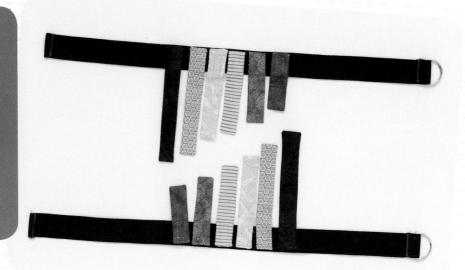

materials

You'll need scraps of 6 different fabrics; label them A—F.

8" x 10" piece of color A for tags

8" x 9" piece of color B for tags

8" x 8" piece of color C for tags

7" x 8" piece of color D for tags

6" x 8" piece of color E for tags

5" x 8" piece of color F for tags

2 yards of 2"-wide nylon webbing for belts (any color)

½ yard of ¾"-wide sew-on Velcro

2 sets of 2" D-rings

Chalk or other fabric marker

CHOOSING COLORS

When you're selecting fabrics, keep in mind that solid colors or tone-on-tone prints will make the tags easier for children to name. If you use multicolor prints, it will be a challenge for both big and little players to call them out. However, having one "rainbow" colored fabric might be fun!

cutting

From *each* of fabrics A—F, cut along the 8" width: 4 strips, 2" x length of fabric*

*A strips will be 10" long, B strips will be 9" long, and so on, down to F strips, which will be 5" long.

making the tags

1. Place two color A strips, 2" x 10", right sides together and raw edges aligned. Using a ½" seam allowance, stitch around three sides, leaving one short end open. Turn the strip right side out and press. Repeat for the remaining color A strips to make two tags of color A. Repeat with the B–F strips to make a total of 12 tags.

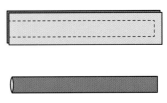

Make 12 total.

making the belt

1. Cut the nylon webbing into two 1-yard lengths, one for each belt. Fold one end of the belt over ½", and then fold this end another ½" so the cut edge is tucked inside. Topstitch the belt on the inner edge of this fold. Adjust your sewing machine so that the stitch length is as small as possible. Sew slowly; the folded edge will be rather thick. I backstitched across the entire length and then stitched again. This will increase the durability of the belt and only takes a few more seconds.

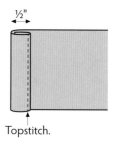

Topstitch.

2. Fold under ½" along the open edge of each tag. To close this opening, sew about ⅛" from the edge along this fold. If you like, you can continue stitching around the perimeter of the entire tag for added durability, but this is optional.

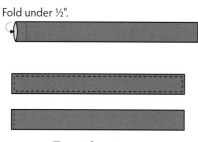

Fold under ½".

Topstitch perimeter
or topstitch end closed.

2. Insert the two D-rings onto the other end of the belt and fold the end of the belt over 1½". Tuck the cut edge under about ½". Sew along this fold as you did before, to secure the edge and the D-rings. Sew an additional row of topstitching as close to the D-rings as possible to further secure them in the belt. This will help keep the belt tighter and prevent slipping and sliding around little waists.

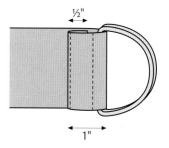

3. Cut the Velcro into 12 pieces, 1½" long. Separate the Velcro pieces into two piles—hooks and loops. Sew the loop strips (the soft side) to the top of each tag, placing the strip ½" from the top and orienting the Velcro vertically so it fits neatly in the center toward the top of the tag. You'll use the hook pieces on the belt.

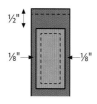

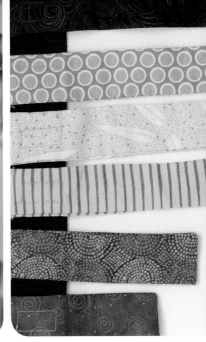

3. Measure 7" from the end with the D-rings and make a mark with a chalk marker. Measure and make a second mark 1¾" from the first. Continue to mark every 1¾" until you have made a total of six marks. These marks will indicate where to place the hook side of the Velcro.

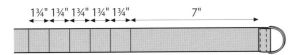

4. Place the Velcro hook pieces (the scratchy sides) on the belt, starting with the first mark at 11". Align the left edge of the Velcro against this first mark, and ¼" down from the top edge of the belt so it's centered on the strap. Make sure the scratchy side is facing up. Machine stitch around all four edges, about ⅛" from the outer edge of the Velcro. Secure the Velcro by backstitching at the beginning and end; it will experience a lot of tugging during its lifetime. Place the next piece of Velcro with the left edge against the next mark and stitch in place. Repeat for the rest of the Velcro pieces on both belts. When you're done, you should have six Velcro ¾" x 1½" rectangles spaced 1" apart and neatly secured to each belt.

5. Attach the tags to the belts using the Velcro strips.

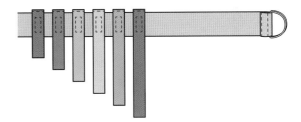

packaging your game

You can store these belts in almost any kind of container. Make a patchwork drawstring bag using matching scraps from the tags (refer to "Drawstring Bag" on page 104). You can also use a cardboard box or plastic container. It would be fun to decoupage an old round cookie tin, which is very inexpensive at secondhand shops—the belts curl up perfectly inside. Playing on the clothing theme, you can also recycle a purse with a zipper. Think outside the game box, literally, and enjoy the many possibilities.

Add a copy of the "How to Play Capture the Tag" game sheet on page 24, and you're done!

Toddlers and Preschoolers

Toddlers will have fun as they explore fastening and unfastening, color matching, and ordering objects by size.

* **Handy Tags:** Have the child remove the tags and refasten them onto the belt. Increase the challenge by securing the belt around the back of a chair so he or she has to stand and reach for them.

* **Colors:** Ask the child to retrieve a specific color. If the child needs help, hold the other belt and point to the color you named.

* **Matching:** Remove the tags from two belts and mix them in a pile on the floor. Ask the child to match them up into color pairs; demonstrate a few to get him or her started. Play again!

* **Sizes:** Remove the tags from one belt and have the child fasten them back onto the belt, in order by size, smallest to largest. Then try largest to smallest.

* **Tag Hunt:** Hang the belt tightly onto the back of a chair and hide the tags so they are still in view but scattered around the room. Call a color and have the child retrieve it and place it onto the belt. Continue until the belt is full. Add a timer for more excitement.

School-Aged Kids

Tag for Tag (2+ players, 1 belt for each player)

A classic game of tag, but with a twist. Each player wears a belt with all tags attached. The youngest player calls a color and the game is on. Each player must capture the tag called from an opponent's belt. Once the tag is caught, the winner calls the next color. The game ends for each player when he or she loses all of his or her tags. The winner is the last one with tags remaining. Increase the challenge by assigning more points to certain tags; the shorter tags are the most difficult to grab.

Capture the Tag (4+ players; 2 teams of 2 or more players; 1 belt for each team)

This game can be played in a large room or open space—indoors or outdoors.

Secure each belt tightly around the back of a chair, a fence, a tree or any other reachable spot, keeping the belts on opposite ends of the playing area. Players on each team line up in front of their belt. When all players are ready, the game begins.

Each team will work together to protect their tags as well as capture the opponent's tags. If someone on the opposite team tags a player, he or she sits down in the spot where tagged and waits to be handed an opponent's captured tag from a teammate in order to re-enter the game. Once someone captures a tag, it can be used to bring one player back into the game. After this, the tag must be discarded into the game bag or box and is out of use. It cannot be used again to free someone else.

The first team to capture all of the opponent's tags wins! For a shorter game, use fewer tags.

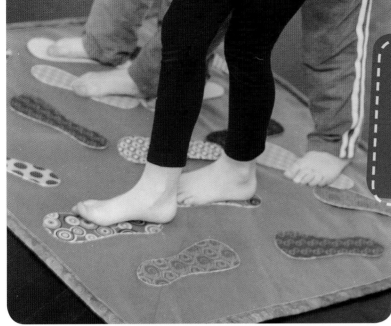

Foot Frenzy

This game is never the same twice. Foot Frenzy keeps the players on their toes, literally! The challenge of balance and coordination, the cooperation it takes to win, and the fun and laughter that it creates makes this game a favorite. Foot Frenzy is quick and easy to construct, and unbelievably fun to play. It's the perfect icebreaker for play dates and kids' groups, as well as a great way to entertain kids at home.

THE GAME CONSISTS OF:

- 40" x 40" floor mat
- 8 pairs of feet
- 8 draw cards
- 1 draw bag

materials

Yardage is based on 42"-wide cotton fabric and 72"-wide premium felt.

1⅝ yards of cotton fabric for floor-mat backing and draw bag*

¼ yard *each* of 8 different-colored prints for feet and draw cards

1¼ yards of premium felt for top of floor mat

1 yard of 20"-wide heavyweight double-sided fusible stabilizer**

⅝ yard of ⅞"- to 1"-wide ribbon for elastic casing of draw bag

¼ yard of ¼"-wide elastic for draw bag

Lightweight cardboard or template plastic

Fabric-marking pen or pencil

Safety pin

Fray preventative (optional)

Fabric should be at least 42" wide to make a self-binding.

**I used Pellon 72F Double-Sided Fusible Ultra Firm Stabilizer.*

cutting

From the cotton fabric, cut:
1 square, 42" x 42"*
2 pieces, 10" x 12"

From the felt, cut:
1 square, 40" x 40"

From the stabilizer, cut:
8 strips, 4" x 20"

From *each* of the ¼-yard prints, cut:
1 strip, 5" x 42" (8 total)

To give you a little more fabric when making a self-binding, you can cut this square larger if your fabric width allows.

making the floor mat

1. Lay the cotton 42" square with the right side down; smooth and iron if necessary. Lay the felt 40" square centered on top. Smooth the felt with your hand from the center out, and pin to hold the two layers together.

2. Topstitch an X over the entire mat. Begin in the center and stitch toward each corner, keeping the felt on top. This will help keep the fabric from shifting and prevent the felt from getting stuck in the feed dogs of your sewing machine.

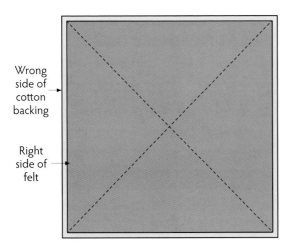

Wrong side of cotton backing

Right side of felt

STITCH AS DESIRED

If you have a free-motion foot for your sewing machine, use it to stitch some fun designs, swirls, and curls on the mat. If your machine is more basic, you can still be creative—use a zigzag stitch and add some gentle curves. Just make sure not to stitch too densely on the mat, because the exposed felt helps the feet stick to the mat while the game is being played.

3. To make a self-binding, place the mat on a flat surface with the felt facing up. Begin near the center of any side and fold in the outer edge of the cotton backing fabric ½", and then fold again so the raw edge is tucked in and the cotton is wrapped over the edge of the felt. Pin in place and fold the remaining edges in around the entire perimeter of the mat. At the corners, fold and tuck in a squared or mitered fashion. Stitch ⅛" from the inner folded edge to secure the binding to the top of the mat. Go slowly at the corners, where the fabric will be thicker. When you reach the beginning of your stitches, backstitch to secure the thread.

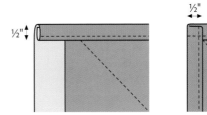

making the feet

Refer to "Fusible Stabilizer" on page 16 as needed.

1. Position a 4" x 20" strip of the fusible stabilizer on the wrong side of one of the print 5" x 42" strips as shown. Fold the strip in half with wrong sides together, sandwiching the stabilizer between the fabric layers. Smooth out any creases and make sure the stabilizer is fully covered by fabric. Following the manufacturer's instructions, iron both sides of the fabric-and-stabilizer sandwich. Let the fabric cool completely before continuing to the next step. Repeat for each of the eight print strips.

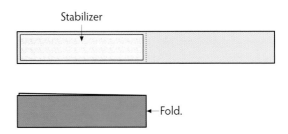

Stabilizer

Fold.

2. Make a template out of cardboard or template plastic using the foot pattern on page 29. Place the heel of the foot template close to one narrow edge of the fused fabric strip. Trace the foot and then trace a second one right in front of it. Place them close together, leaving 2" excess at the opposite end of the strip for the draw card. Double-check that the fabric has fused completely to the stabilizer. Apply the iron again if needed. Repeat for each fused fabric strip.

2" excess

3. Using sharp scissors, cut out each foot. Cut a 2" x 4" rectangle from the leftover end of each fabric strip to make the draw cards.

NEAT FEET

If you don't want to see your creations develop "personality" over the years, fray preventative will keep the edges clean and free from fraying threads. I skipped this step and our feet have a fun bit of fray around the edges, but the glue from the fusible stabilizer has kept them intact and ready for many more years of play.

making the draw bag

1. Layer the two cotton 10" x 12" rectangles with right sides together. Align the raw edges and pin. Sew around three sides using a ½" seam allowance and leaving one 10" side open.

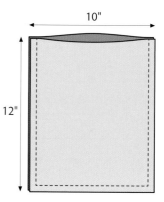

10"

12"

2. Fold the edge of the opening ½" to the wrong side. Fold another ½" to make a hem. Pin and topstitch ¼" from the inner folded edge.

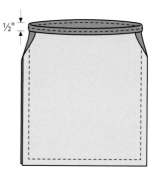

½"

3. Turn the bag right side out and refer to step 3 of "Elastic Draw Bag" on page 107 to complete the bag.

packaging your game

The mat folds up nicely into a square with all of the accessories tucked inside. Repurpose an old purse or bag, decorate a large lidded box, or construct a quick drawstring bag for light and easy storage (refer to "Drawstring Bag" on page 104). If you're looking for absolute simplicity, hem the raw ends of a ribbon and use it to tie the mat bundle when folded up.

Add a copy of the "How to Play Foot Frenzy" game sheet on page 30, and you're done!

Foot

FOOT FRENZY

Toddlers and Preschoolers

Explore matching, identify colors, and engage in some basic coordination activities. These versions can be used with or without the mat. There's no winning or losing, just quizzing on colors, patterns, and matching.

* **Color Matching:** Lay out one foot from each pair, and then stack the corresponding feet in a pile. Pull from the pile, hand the foot to the child, and ask the child to name the color. Next, have the child find the matching foot. Continue with the rest of the feet until all pairs are matched!

* **Footpath:** Create a path around the room with the feet and have the child walk the path, being careful not to step off the feet. This works best on carpet or a rug, where the feet will not slip. To increase the challenge, lay out the draw cards around the path and have the child collect them as you call out the colors you want him or her to retrieve.

* **Bitty Foot Frenzy:** Place all of the feet on the mat and have the child find and stand on one color foot. Continue with each of the colors.

School-Aged Kids

Setting Up the Game

Lay the mat felt side up. Divide the feet equally among two to four players (pass any extras to the youngest players). Standing about five feet from the mat, take turns to toss the feet onto the mat. The player with the most feet that land on the mat will draw first. Players collect any feet that did not land on the mat and toss again until all feet land on the felt portion of the mat. Now choose a game!

Foot Friends (cooperative fun for 2 to 4 players)

The first player draws a card from the draw bag and places his or her feet on the matching feet on the mat. Discard this card into a pile; *do not put it back in the bag.* The next player draws a card from the draw bag and places his or her feet on the matching feet on the mat. Continue with each player, starting back with the first player when everyone has drawn and stepped onto the mat. With the second draw, players move to a different pair of feet. In this game, teamwork is the only way to conquer these tricky feet. Players can hold onto each other for support in order to win as a team. Play continues until the draw bag is empty, or *one* member of the team falls. If no one falls, your team succeeded!

Foot Frenzy (competitive fun for 2 to 4 players)

The first player selects a card from the draw bag and places his or her feet on the matching feet on the mat. *Return this card to the bag.* The next player draws a card from the draw bag, places his or her feet on the matching feet on the mat, and returns the card to the bag as well. Continue drawing in order. If a player draws a card that matches feet another player is already standing on, both players stand on one foot until it is again their turn to draw and move to another pair of feet. The player who drew the card chooses which foot to stand on. If a player falls, game over for that player. When everyone falls, play again!

Monster Ball

Monster Ball brings the enjoyment of the carnival home to you. This game has stood the test of time. Kids have the chance to focus on building their hand-eye coordination skills, while taking turns and tracking points. Try it blindfolded for added challenge. This project requires very little sewing and would be easy to personalize with countless other themes. Enjoy a few rounds—scoring points is not as easy as it looks.

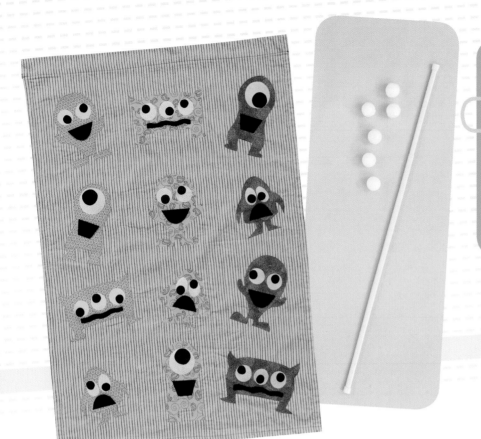

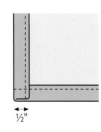

THE GAME CONSISTS OF:

- 28" x 40" panel with 12 monsters
- hanging rod
- 6 sticky balls

materials

Yardage is based on 42"-wide fabric.

1¼ yards of cotton fabric for background panel

¼ yard *each* of 3 different-colored fabrics for monsters

⅛ yard of white solid for eyes

⅛ yard of black solid for pupils

2 yards of 17"-wide lightweight, sewable fusible web

1 yard of 2"-wide black sew-on Velcro

24 *no-sew*, adhesive Velcro ⅝" dots

6 ping-pong balls (found at any discount, department, or sporting store)

1 spring tension curtain rod to fit a standard 32" to 36" doorway

Lightweight cardboard or template plastic

Fabric marking pen or pencil

cutting

From the background fabric, cut:
1 panel, 30" x length of fabric

making the background panel

1. Trim and square up the 30"-wide ends of the background panel if necessary, so that the corners are 90°.

2. Place the background panel on a flat surface, right side down, and fold the edge ½" to the wrong side. Fold another ½" to make a hem. Pin and topstitch about ⅛" from the inner folded edge. Continue around three sides of the fabric panel, leaving one 30" edge unfolded. Fold the corners in squarely and secure them as you go.

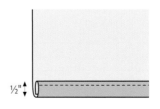

3. Fold the unsewn 30" edge ½" to the wrong side, and then fold 1½". Pin and topstitch as you did the other sides. This will create the hanging sleeve for the curtain rod.

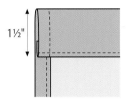

preparing the monsters

Refer to "Fusible Web" on page 14 for more details regarding this technique.

1. Using the patterns on pages 35–38, trace one of each monster onto the paper side of the fusible web. Leave about ½" between each monster. Cut loosely around the group of monsters.

2. Following the manufacturer's instructions, fuse the web to the wrong side of one of the ¼-yard pieces of fabric for monsters. Allow the fabric to cool, and then cut out the monsters on the drawn lines.

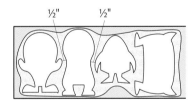

3. Repeat steps 1 and 2 for each of the remaining two ¼-yard pieces of fabric. You should have one of each monster in every color.

4. Trace the monster eyes onto the fusible web and fuse it to the white fabric in the same manner. Repeat to fuse the monster pupils to the black fabric. Cut out the eyes and pupils.

5. Separate the 2"-wide black Velcro and set aside the hook portion (it is scratchy and more difficult to sew). Use the soft loop side for the mouths. Make templates from cardboard or template plastic using the mouth patterns on pages 35–38. Trace the mouth patterns onto the smooth side of the Velcro using a white marker, and cut them out.

assembling the monster panel

1. Peel the paper backing from the monsters and arrange them on the right side of the background panel in three vertical rows of four monsters each. Be sure to orient the hanging sleeve at the top, and make sure the fusible-web side is facing the background panel. Evenly distribute the monsters as shown, keeping the same-colored monsters in the same vertical row. If you are like me, just eyeball their positions. If you are type A, then you may want to get a ruler out to measure the space in between to make sure they are evenly placed. I guarantee that the kids playing the game will never check your work.

5. Continue to fuse each monster and its corresponding eyes onto the background panel until they're all attached. Once the fabric has completely cooled, you can check for any missed edges and go back over them with a hot iron. *It's important that you always wait until the fabric is completely cooled to recheck; only then is the adhesive fully dried.*

6. Place each monster mouth on its appropriate monster and sew the black Velcro ⅛" from the edge using the shortest stitch length possible to secure it firmly to the body. This mouth will see a lot of wear with the Velcro balls being tugged off of them, so be sure to do a secure backstitch at the beginning and end.

2. Prepare the eyes and pupils for fusing by removing the paper backing and pairing them in the appropriate combinations. You'll want to add them to the monsters after fusing the bodies in place, while they're still warm.

3. Preheat your iron and choose your first monster. Remove the pins and iron the monster body following the manufacturer's instructions for the fusible web that you're using.

4. Select the appropriate white eyes (or eye) and place them, fusible side down, onto the monster. Fuse with an iron. Do the same for the black pupils. The more off-center and goofy they look, the more the kids love them (and somehow, this makes them look even friendlier).

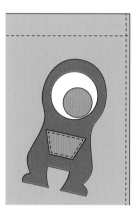

preparing the balls

Apply four Velcro dots to each ping-pong ball. Use the hook (scratchy) side of the dots only.

I like to use the analogy of the globe for choosing the position of each dot. Consider the ball a globe of the world, apply a dot at each compass point: north, south, east, and west (top, bottom, and one on each side).

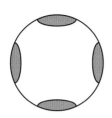

packaging your game

With this game, the curtain rod makes it an unusual shape and size for packaging. I suggest you decorate a cardboard tube (like the ones posters or drawings are shipped in), or sew a long, narrow, fabric drawstring bag (refer to "Drawstring Bag" on page 104). You can slip the rolled-up game and ping-pong balls inside.

Add a copy of the "How to Play Monster Ball" game sheet on page 39, and you're done!

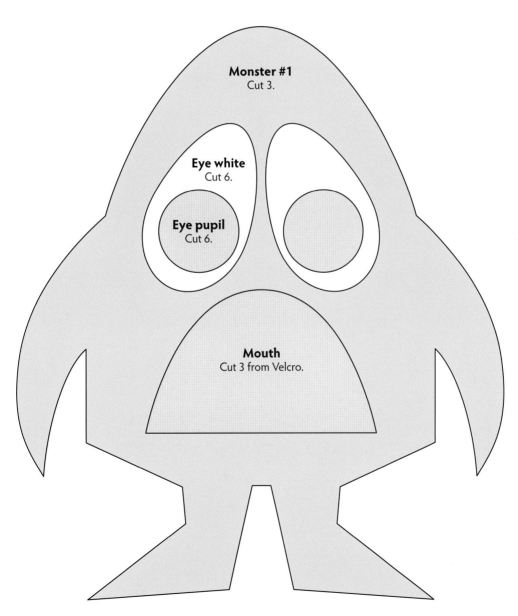

Monster #1
Cut 3.

Eye white
Cut 6.

Eye pupil
Cut 6.

Mouth
Cut 3 from Velcro.

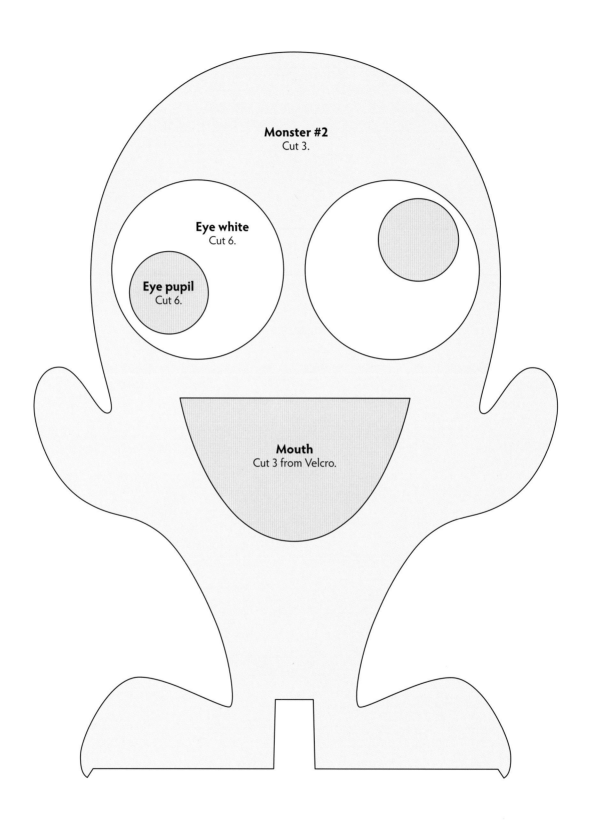

Monster #2
Cut 3.

Eye white
Cut 6.

Eye pupil
Cut 6.

Mouth
Cut 3 from Velcro.

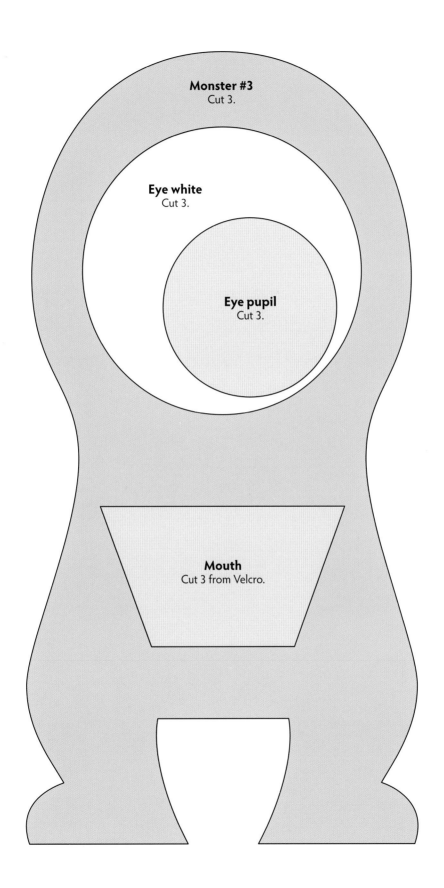

Monster #3
Cut 3.

Eye white
Cut 3.

Eye pupil
Cut 3.

Mouth
Cut 3 from Velcro.

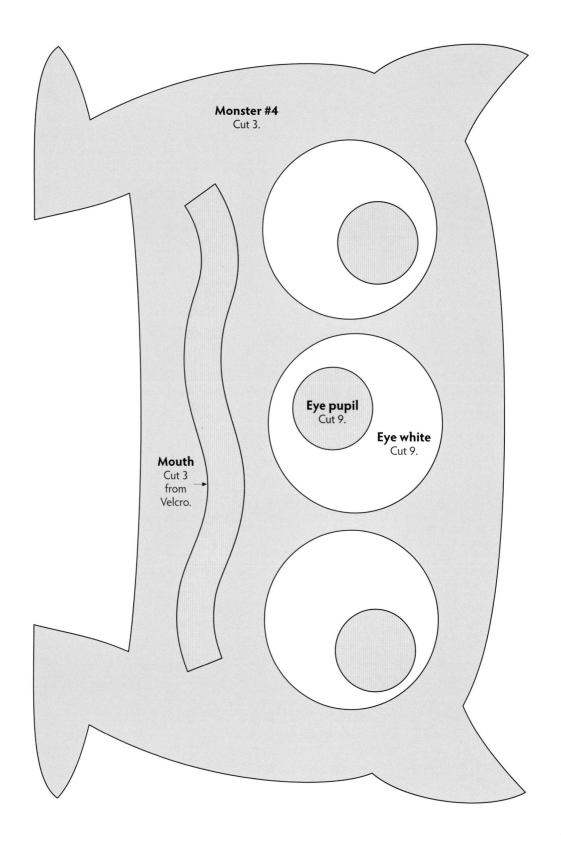

Monster #4
Cut 3.

Mouth
Cut 3 from Velcro.

Eye pupil
Cut 9.

Eye white
Cut 9.

Toddlers and Preschoolers

Here are some great opportunities for practicing dynamic reaching, early fine-motor skills, as well as basic counting.

* For children who are walking, hang this game in a doorway with the bottom edge flush with the floor, and the door closed behind the fabric to give it stability. For sitters and crawlers, lay the game flat on the floor with monsters facing up.

* **Monster Munch:** The monsters are hungry! Ask the child to feed the monsters by placing the Velcro balls onto the mouths of the monsters. To add challenge, specify which monster is hungry and how much he eats (i.e. "The yellow monster at the bottom wants two yummy balls!"). Once all of the monsters have been fed, have the child reach and retrieve all of the "leftovers," and then play again. To challenge balance and coordination, pick out a monster that is higher and requires some reaching.

School-Aged Kids

Monster Ball (for 2 to 4 players)

Hang the monster game panel securely in a walkway or doorframe, at the same height as the tallest player. The door can be open or closed.

Starting with the youngest, each player chooses which set of four monsters will be his or hers. Next, players stand in front of the game and take the same number of steps backward as their age (four years old equals four large steps backward). This will be where each player throws.

One at a time, using all six balls, players throw the balls at their colored monsters, trying to get them to stick to the mouths. The more balls players can feed their monsters, the more points they receive! If a player gets two balls in one monster's mouth, he or she gets double the points; that means four points for two balls. If a player gets three balls in one, then he or she gets triple, or nine points for that throw (four balls would get 16 points!). If a player's ball accidentally feeds another player's monster, he or she must subtract that ball from his or her score. Once a player has thrown all six balls and added up the score, the next player goes. The first player to reach 15 points wins!

Pancake Party

These pancakes will entertain the whole family! The multiple layers of felt textures will enthrall toddlers. The preschool games encourage social skills and imaginative play, as well as memory and basic math concepts. School-aged games encourage balance, spatial awareness, gross motor coordination, and decision making. Even parents can join in the fun of playing Pancake Party.

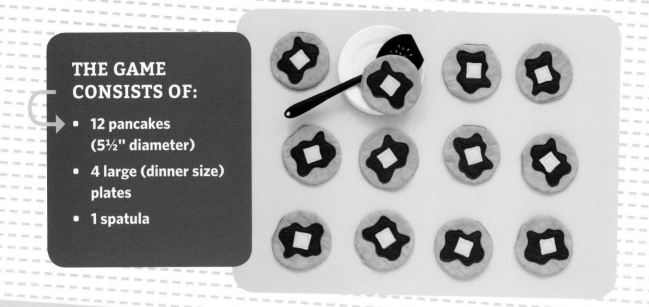

THE GAME CONSISTS OF:

- **12 pancakes (5½" diameter)**
- **4 large (dinner size) plates**
- **1 spatula**

materials

Yardage is based on 42"-wide fabric.

1 yard of light-brown solid or tone-on-tone for pancakes

3 pieces, 8" x 11", of dark-brown felt for syrup

8" x 11" piece of yellow felt for butter

21" x 28" piece of quilt batting

Dark-brown acrylic paint or fabric paint

Small sponge

Lightweight cardboard or template plastic

Spatula and 4 large (dinner size) plastic stackable plates*

*Check for these at a grocery or discount store.

cutting

Make templates for the pancake and syrup using the patterns on page 44. Refer to the cutting guides at right.

From the light-brown solid or tone-on-tone, cut:
12 pancakes from folded fabric (24 total)

From the batting, cut:
12 pancakes

From the yellow felt, cut:
24 squares, 1½" x 1½"

From the brown felt, cut:
12 syrup pieces

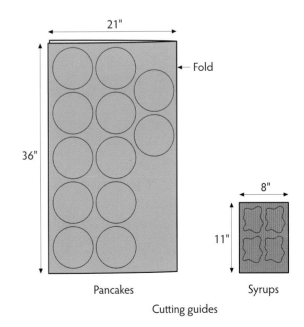

Cutting guides

making the pancakes

When making the pancakes, try to make them all look identical. Some of the games include penalties for the burnt pancake, and you don't want the players to be able to spot it during the game.

1. Center a syrup piece on the right side of a light-brown circle and stitch it onto the pancake ⅛" from the edge of the syrup. Use a darning foot if available. (Refer to "Free-Motion Stitching" on page 13.) Repeat for the top circle of all 12 pancakes.

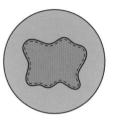

2. For the butter slices, stack and topstitch two yellow 1½" squares onto the center of each syrup piece.

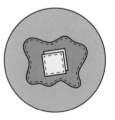

3. Place a pancake with syrup and butter on a bottom pancake circle, right sides together. Place a circle of quilt batting on top of the pancake with syrup and butter. Add a few pins to hold the layers together if desired.

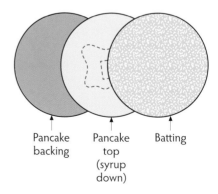

Pancake backing   Pancake top (syrup down)   Batting

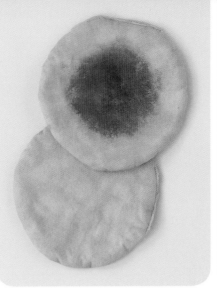
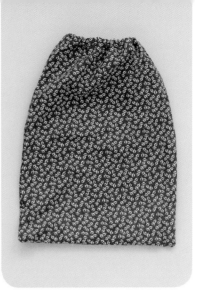

4. With the batting on top, sew around the perimeter of the pancake layers using a ½" seam allowance and leaving 2" unsewn. Repeat for the 12 pancakes.

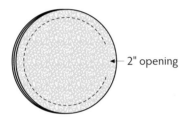

← 2" opening

5. Turn the pancakes right side out. Hand or machine sew the openings closed. For hand stitching, refer to "Ladder Stitch" on page 17 for detailed instructions. You can also use a blind stitch or slip stitch. Press the pancakes if necessary, being cautious with the iron on the felt.

6. To make the burnt pancake, use a sponge to dab some dark-brown paint on the bottom center of one pancake. Leave an inch around the edge unpainted; let the paint dry. You should not be able to see any of the paint when this pancake is right side up.

packaging your game

This game is very portable and can be packaged in a number of ways. Repurposing a picnic basket or a plastic cake carrier would be a fun way to store this game. You can also make a drawstring bag using classic red-and-white checkered tablecloth fabric (refer to "Drawstring Bag" on page 104).

Add a copy of the "How to Play Pancake Party" game sheet on page 45, and you're done!

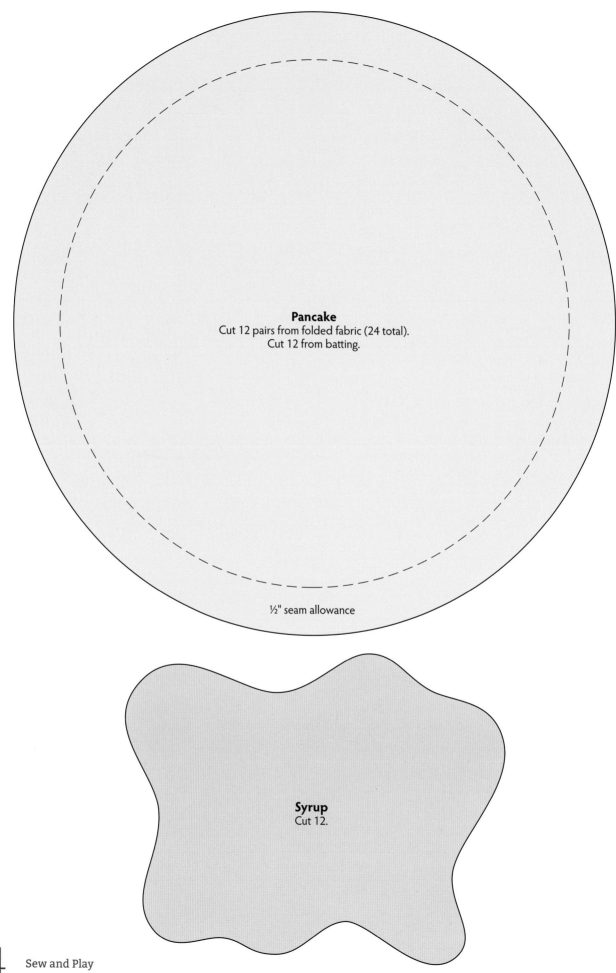

Pancake
Cut 12 pairs from folded fabric (24 total).
Cut 12 from batting.

½" seam allowance

Syrup
Cut 12.

How to Play
PANCAKE PARTY

Toddlers and Preschoolers

* **Pancake Play:** Have the child stack the pancakes, explore their textures, toss them, or just pull the stack apart!

* **Pancake House:** Imaginary play is great fun at this age. Create a restaurant with a table, chairs, a tablecloth, and other props. Pull out a kitchen apron for each child and let them take your order. Have them go to the "kitchen," count out the number of pancakes you ordered by memory, and serve them onto your plate using the spatula. If served the burnt pancake, send it back and ask for more!

School-Aged Kids

Pancake Shuffle (2 players)

Cooperative fun! Standing 8 to 10 feet apart, one player tosses all of the pancakes with the spatula, and the other player catches them on his or her plate. When the pancake is caught, set it aside or keep it on the plate for an additional challenge. If the pancake falls off, it doesn't count! Switch places. The duo wins if together they can catch a total of six pancakes on their plates.

Pancake Shuffle (3 to 5 players)

Competitive fun! One player takes the spatula and pancakes; the other players each take a plate. Standing 10 steps away from the thrower, each player holds out a plate and tries to catch pancakes as the first player tosses them, underhanded, using the spatula. If the pancake slides off, it doesn't count. The player with the most pancakes wins!

Blindfold the thrower if he or she is showing favoritism. If pancakes slide off the plates too easily or if younger players are having a hard time, use larger plates or add a circle of non-slip shelf liner.

Pancake Toss (2 to 5 players)

Place plates randomly on the floor, approximately 12" apart. Take five steps backward for the first round. Each player tosses all 12 pancakes with the spatula and scores one point for every pancake landing on a plate. No points are given if any part of the pancake is touching the floor, because we don't eat food off the floor! The burnt pancake equals two points since it will get the player an extra pancake and a waiter's apology!

For the next round, the players take 10 steps back. To increase the challenge, increase the distance from the plates (15 steps, and so on) for each subsequent round. The game is completed on the round when no one gets any pancakes on a plate. Tally the points; the highest score wins.

Burnt Pancake (2 to 4 players)

Spread the pancakes on a table or floor, syrup side up, shuffling them well. Players sit in a circle around the pancakes and each player has a plate. During a turn, the player takes as many pancakes as desired, one at a time and using the spatula, checking the bottom for the burnt pancake each time. The object of the game is to get as many pancakes as possible. If a player picks the burnt pancake, the game ends, and the player with the most pancakes wins. The more pancakes you take in a turn, the closer you get to winning . . . or to the burnt pancake!

Horse Race

Horse Race is a simple and unique puzzle game that loves to travel and offers an enjoyable opportunity for kids to practice taking turns, enhance essential fine motor skills, and sharpen visual perception. Pass the saddlebag around to see who gets the lucky draw and can get their horse to the finish line first. Horse Race is an easy and enjoyable project that can be completed in an afternoon.

THE GAME CONSISTS OF:

- **4 horse panels (11" x 17" each)**
- **1 saddlebag**

materials

Yardage is based on 42"-wide fabric.

⅞ yard of cotton fabric for backing

⅓ yard *each* of 2 prints for binding

½ yard of brown fabric for saddlebag (brown ultrasuede has a great faux leather feel)

4 fat quarters (18" x 21") of assorted prints for the panels

4 pieces, 10" x 14", of marine vinyl in assorted colors for horse bodies*

36" x 24" piece of quilt batting

1 skein *each* of embroidery floss in 4 colors that coordinate with the horse bodies

4 buttons, 1¼" diameter, for horse bodies

8 buttons, 1" diameter, for horse legs

12 buttons, ¾" diameter, for horse heads, necks, and tails

Lightweight cardboard or template plastic

1 yard of ⅞"-wide ribbon for casing on saddlebag

10" of ¼"-wide elastic

Machine upholstery needle and thread

X-acto knife or rotary cutter and mat

Black permanent marker

Washable marker

Rustproof safety pins for pin basting

11" of western-style faux leather fringe (optional)

*A ⅛-yard cut of each will also work.

PROJECT OPTIONS

Simplify. *If you want to make project easier or quicker, omit the quilt batting, backing, and binding. Refer to "Foundations" on page 110 for detailed instructions.*

Alternate Themes. *Does your little one have a favorite animal or toy? Turn this fun puzzle game into "Turtle Race" or "Race Cars." See "Alternate Themes" on page 12 for more ideas.*

Other Fabrics. *If you're looking for an alternative to vinyl, use felt for the horses. Or use a heavyweight one-sided fusible stabilizer, fused with cotton fabric to create an 8" x 10" rectangle to cut the four puzzle pieces. Dab fray preventative on the edges and in the buttonhole to finish. Refer to "Fusible Stabilizer" on page 16 as needed.*

Buttons. *Feel free to use slightly different sizes of buttons. Just check the pattern pieces to make sure the buttonhole won't need to be wider than the puzzle piece it will be used for.*

cutting

Make templates for the horse puzzle pieces using the patterns on page 52.

From *each* of the fat quarters, cut:
1 rectangle, 12" x 18"

From the fabric for backing, cut:
2 strips, 12" x 42"; crosscut into 4 rectangles,
   12" x 18"

From *each* of the prints for binding, cut:
4 strips, 2" x 11" (8 total)
4 strips, 2" x 20" (8 total)

From the batting, cut:
4 rectangles, 12" x 18"

From *each* piece of vinyl, cut:
1 *each* of the 5 horse puzzle pieces

From the brown fabric, cut:
2 rectangles, 12" x 18"

making the background panels

1. Place one of the 12" x 18" backing rectangles on a flat surface, wrong side up. Place a 12" x 18" piece of batting on top, and then place a print 12" x 18" background rectangle on top of that, right side up, as if layering a quilt. Pin the layers together using safety pins. Repeat for all of the backing, batting, and background rectangles.

2. Machine quilt the pinned sandwich in any pattern you are comfortable with. Using the darning foot on my sewing machine, I like to stitch free-motion swirls, because they're easy and whimsical. Repeat for all four panels.

3. Trim and square up the edges and corners of the panels to measure 11" x 17" You want a clean, straight edge for attaching the binding.

4. Place the 2" x 11" binding strips on the *backing side* of a panel, right sides together, aligning the raw edges with the short edges of the panel. Pin and sew ½" from the edge. Press the seam allowances toward the strips. Trim the short edges of the strips even with the panel, if necessary. Place the 2" x 20" binding strips on the panel, right sides together, aligning the raw edges with the remaining two sides of the panel. Pin and sew ½" from the edge and press the seam allowances toward the strips.

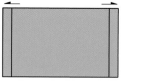

5. Flip the panel right side up. Starting in the center of any side, fold the binding over the top of the panel, keeping it tight with the edge. Fold the raw edge of the binding under ½", and pin in place. Continue around the entire perimeter of the panel, and then sew ⅛" from the inner folded edge to secure the binding. Fold and sew the corners in a squared or mitered fashion. Repeat for each panel.

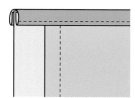

preparing the horse puzzle pieces

1. Organize your horse puzzle pieces by color. Center one button onto each horse puzzle piece and use a washable marker to mark a dot at the top and bottom of the button. (Refer to the "Materials" on page 47 for button sizes.) Set the button aside and draw a line from one mark to the other to connect the dots and mark the buttonhole.

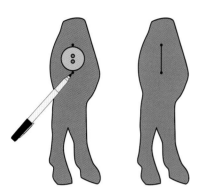

2. Before you cut, be sure that there is enough excess vinyl or fabric on all sides of the buttonhole to allow for the tugging that these puzzle pieces will endure. If the buttonhole looks like it will be too long when you mark it, choose a smaller button and make a shorter hole. There is no redo on cutting the buttonhole, but there should be enough extra vinyl to cut a new puzzle piece if needed. Using an X-acto knife or small rotary cutter on a mat, very carefully slice along the marked line to create the buttonhole, making sure you don't cut too far.

3. Cut a 1½" x 5" rectangle from a scrap of cardboard. Cut a slit in the cardboard about ¼" from the end and about ¼" long. This will be a guide for making the horse mane and tail. The slit will secure the tail end of the embroidery floss. (Cereal boxes work great for this.)

4. Wrap the embroidery floss around the *width* of the cardboard from top to bottom until the cardboard is covered in floss. Leave an edge to hold onto.

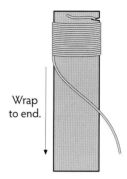

Wrap to end.

5. Remove the tail of the floss from the slit in the cardboard. Gently slide the cardboard out and lay the "hair" across the top edge of the neck puzzle piece, as shown on the pattern. With an upholstery needle in your sewing machine, topstitch the floss in place, being careful not to let any of the floss get loose. If you miss some threads, repeat with additional topstitching. Cut the bottom loops to create a natural-looking mane.

6. Using the same cardboard template, cut a slit in the short end as shown. Wrap the same color embroidery floss *lengthwise* around the template 8 to 10 times, or more if you prefer a thicker tail. Cut the end at the same side you began wrapping and gently pull the cardboard out of the wound floss. The two loose ends should be on the same edge.

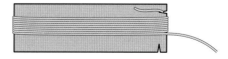

7. Measure in ⅞" (or the diameter of your smallest button, plus ⅛") from the end of the tail that has no loose or cut ends. Cut a 6" length of embroidery floss, tie it around the tail, and knot tightly at this point. This will create the button loop for attaching the tail to the horse. Test the opening with the button and make sure it slides through. Wrap both ends of the excess around the tail in opposite directions two to three times and knot tightly again. Then smooth the ends to blend with the tail. For added strength, you can topstitch just below this knotted area on the tail, or put a dab of craft glue on the knot. Cut the loops at the bottom of the tail, the opposite end of where you created the button loop.

8. Select a leftover scrap of vinyl in any color, and trace one horse head pattern onto it. Cut this out and color this piece black using a permanent marker. There's no need for a buttonhole. This will be the "Black Stallion" piece for a variation on the game.

attaching the buttons

1. Arrange the horse puzzle pieces on top of each corresponding panel, centering them as much as possible. Leave about ⅛" between each of the puzzle pieces. Mark the placement of the buttons: hold the puzzle piece to avoid shifting, insert a marker through the very center of the buttonhole, and mark a small dot onto the background panel. This is where you will sew the button. Repeat for each puzzle piece. Mark one final button ½" to the left of the horse's rump. This is for the tail.

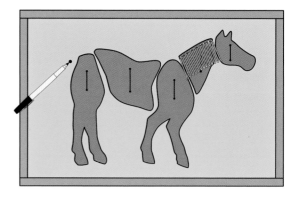

2. Remove the puzzle pieces and sew the appropriate button on each marked spot. Refer to the puzzle pieces to make sure you sew the correct size button in the correct spot. Sew buttons on very securely so they will not end up in little mouths or noses.

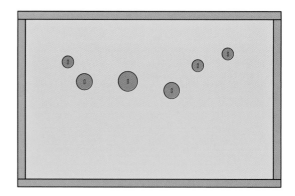

3. Attach all of the puzzle pieces onto each completed panel.

making the saddlebag

1. Layer the two brown 12" x 18" rectangles with right sides together. To add the fringe at the bottom, sandwich it between the two layers, aligning the straight edge with the bottom edges of the rectangles. Pin, and sew the fringe in place. (Keep the loose fringe oriented upward so it is not sewn into the seam.) Stitch around three sides of the layered rectangles, leaving one 12" side unstitched for the top opening.

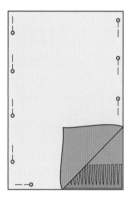 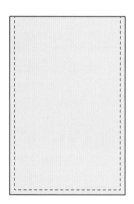

2. Fold the edge of the opening ½" to the wrong side. Fold another ½" to make a hem. Pin and topstitch ⅛" from the inner folded edge.

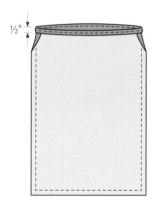

3. Turn the bag right side out and refer to step 3 of "Elastic Draw Bag" on page 107 to complete the bag.

4. The saddlebag will hold all of the game parts if you roll up the horse panels for storage. Add a copy of the "How to Play Horse Race" game sheet on page 53, and you're done!

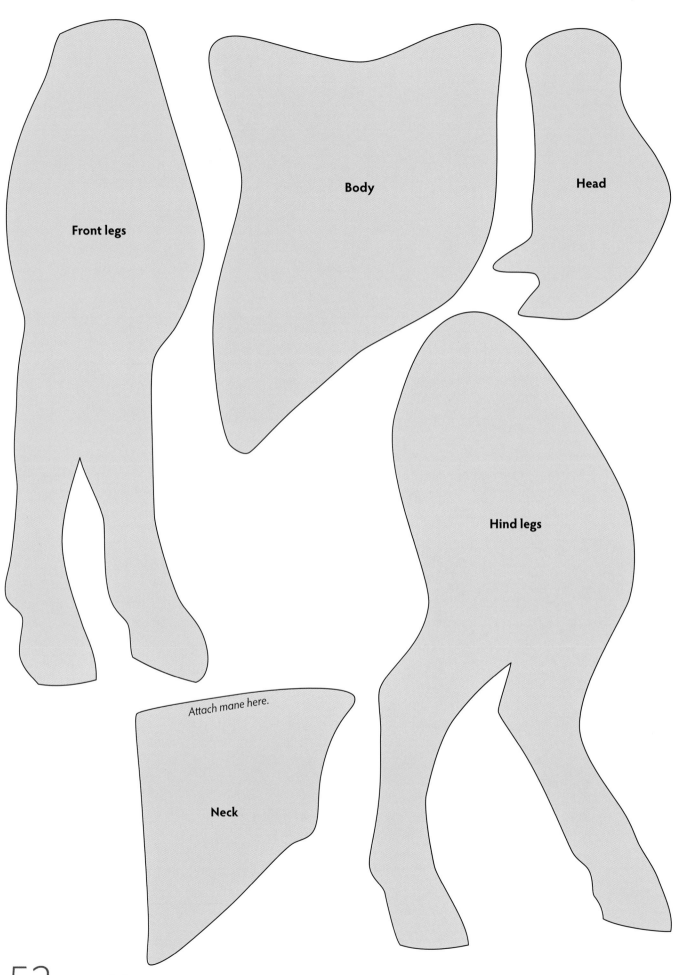

Front legs

Body

Head

Hind legs

Attach mane here.

Neck

HORSE RACE ↩

Toddlers and Preschoolers

This game is a great early cognitive challenge, as well as good practice for developing visual perception skills. In addition, it encourages fine motor and life skills all through a bit of fun.

* **Button up:** For the wee ones, have them focus on buttoning and unbuttoning, guiding them to where the pieces go, and helping with the buttoning as needed.

* **Build-a-Horse:** For children in later developmental stages, give them an assembled horse panel and have them unbutton all of the pieces. Ask them to assemble them in the shape of the horse, next to the puzzle. Next, have them put the pieces back on the puzzle in the correct order. This is a greater challenge to cognition, memory, and visual perception.

School-Aged Kids

Horse Race (2 to 4 players)

Each player picks a horse panel, and then unbuttons and removes all of the horse pieces from the panel, placing them into the saddlebag. Before beginning, each player takes a turn shaking the saddlebag, mixing the various colors. The game begins with the youngest player drawing a piece from the saddlebag without looking. If the piece matches the color of that player's horse, the player can button it onto his or her panel. Passing the saddlebag clockwise, the rest of the players draw. If a player draws a piece that doesn't belong to his horse, he places it back in the bag and passes it to the next player. Only one draw per turn, and players are not allowed to peek in the bag. If caught, they lose a piece of their horse back into the bag. The first player to complete his or her horse wins!

Note: If there are only two to three players, increase the challenge by adding all of the horse pieces to the saddlebag, even those that will not be played. Little minds can utilize the process of elimination as their choice of pieces narrows.

Horse Thief (2 to 4 players)

Play the game as instructed above, but with the addition of the "Black Stallion" horse piece. If a player draws this piece at any time in the game, then a horse thief came in the night and stole from the herd. The player must place a piece of his or her horse back in the saddlebag. After it's drawn, discard the "Black Stallion" piece.

The Great Horse Derby (2 to 4 players)

This game is fast and fun. Remove all horse pieces and place them in one pile in front of all players. Count to three and off they go! Players race to grab their pieces from the pile and assemble their horses correctly. The first one to the "finish line" wins!

Crab Crawl

Crab Crawl offers a great ocean adventure with adorable characters, and an opportunity for kids to count sand dollars as their crabs make their way to the shore. Fun for all ages and easy to construct, this is a delightful game for a rainy day and it travels well on family vacations to the beach.

THE GAME CONSISTS OF:

- 16" x 90" ocean-and-beach mat
- 4 crabs
- 16 sand dollars
- 1 die

materials

Yardage is based on 42"-wide cotton fabric, 54"-wide tulle, and 72"-wide premium felt. Fat quarters measure 18" x 21".

1⅝ yards of cotton fabric for backing and pocket of mat

⅓ yard of red fabric for crab bodies

1 fat quarter *each* of 4 assorted blue fabrics for water

1 fat quarter of tan fabric for beach

½ yard of white tulle or other netting*

⅛ yard of premium white felt for crab eyes and sand dollars

10" x 13" piece of premium red felt for crab pincers, legs, and eyestalks

9" x 12" piece or scraps of black felt for crab pupils

4 scraps, 1½" x 2½", in different-colored fabrics for bow ties

18" x 94" piece of quilt batting**

8 ounces of fiberfill

1-pound bag of plastic pellets

Black embroidery floss or black permanent marker

44" of parachute or other cording for tying the mat closed

Fabric glue

1 die

Lightweight cardboard or template plastic

Fabric-marking pen or pencil

Other nettings may come in different widths; you'll need enough to cut 2 pieces, 10½" x 18" each.

**You can piece together two or more pieces of 18"-wide batting with a gentle whip stitch to make the length needed.*

cutting

Make templates for the crab parts and sand dollars using the patterns on page 60.

From *each* of the 4 blue fat quarters*, cut:
2 rectangles, 10½" x 18" (8 total)

From the white tulle, cut:
2 rectangles, 10½" x 18"

From the tan fabric, cut:
1 square, 18" x 18"

From the fabric for backing, cut:
2 rectangles, 18" x 46", on *the lengthwise grain*
1 rectangle, 9" x 12"

From the red fabric, cut:
4 crabs from folded fabric (8 total)

From *each* of the 4 assorted scraps, cut:
1 bow tie

From the red felt, cut:
8 eyestalks
8 legs
8 pincers

From the white felt, cut:
16 sand dollars
8 eyes

From the black felt, cut:
8 pupils

*If your fat quarters are a little scant, it's okay if the rectangles are a bit smaller than the sizes listed. Just cut all of your pieces to the same dimensions or trim the edges of the mat after assembling.

making the mat

1. Arrange the eight blue 10½" x 18" rectangles in a row along their long edges as shown, with right sides up and alternating the different fabrics. Place a tulle 10½" x 18" rectangle on top of the third and sixth rectangle from the left end. Pin the tulle in place.

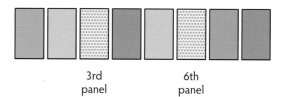

3rd panel   6th panel

2. With right sides together, pin and sew the panels along their long edges, using a ½" seam allowance and including the two panels with tulle on top. Press the seam allowances open or to one side, being cautious when ironing the tulle. Lay a pressing cloth or scrap fabric over the tulle to make sure you don't melt or scorch it.

3. Place the tan 18" square on a flat surface. Measure and mark 4" from the top right corner. From this mark, cut a wavy line through the fabric, ending at the bottom right corner, as shown. Cut this freehand for a natural look to depict the ocean washing up onto the shore.

4"

4. With right sides up, place the trimmed tan square along one short end of the pieced blue panel, overlapping at least 1" and covering the blue panel along the entire short edge. Align the edges with the blue panels, continuing to make straight edges along the mat. Pin and topstitch the tan piece onto the blue panel, using a wide zigzag stitch and a thread color that matches the tan fabric. Stitch the edge again using a satin stitch (a zigzag stitch set at the shortest length) for the best coverage.

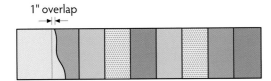

1" overlap

OPTIONAL SEA FOAM

Layer bunched-up scraps of tulle along the "shoreline" and stitch them in place to create a three-dimensional effect of waves leaving foam on the beach.

5. To make the backing for the mat, layer the two 18" x 46" backing rectangles with right sides together. Sew along one short edge using a ½" seam allowance. Press the seam allowances open or to one side.

6. To make the pocket, fold one short edge of the 9" x 12" backing rectangle ½" to the wrong side. Fold another ½" to make a hem. Stitch in place, about ⅛" from the inner folded edge.

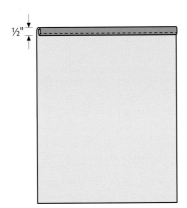

½"

7. Fold the remaining three edges under ½" and press.

8. Measure 6" from the short edge of the backing from step 5, and place the pocket on the backing, right sides up. Center the pocket and

pin in place. Stitch along the three folded edges, securing the pocket to the backing and leaving the hemmed edge open at the top.

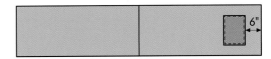

6"

9. Layer the ocean-and-beach panel and backing with right sides together. Trim the backing to the same size as the panel if necessary. Place the batting on top, as if layering a quilt. The backing should be on the bottom and the ocean panel should be in the middle.

10. If you're using parachute cord, refer to "Parts from Parachute Cord" on page 19 and seal the ends to prevent fraying. Fold the 44" length of cording in half and insert it between the two fabric layers as shown, centered in the middle of the pocket end of the backing. The folded part should be visible on the outside of the sandwich, and two long tails should be between the layers inside. Pin the three layers together and sew along the perimeter, using a ½" seam allowance and leaving a 6" opening at the end opposite the cording. As you sew, make sure the loose ends of the cording don't get sewn into the seam.

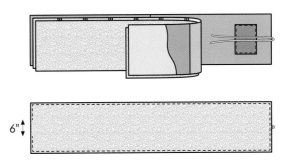

6"

11. Turn the mat right side out and press. Topstitch the opening closed ¼" from the edge.

12. Quilt the mat in whatever fashion you like. Simple curved lines imitate waves and they are easy to sew with any sewing machine.

making the crabs

1. On the right side of four crab bodies, mark the location of the bow tie and the mouth.

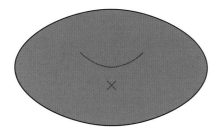

2. Double thread your needle with six strands of black embroidery floss (12 strands total) and knot the end. Starting at one end of the mouth, sew a running stitch along the entire length of the line (refer to "Running Stitch" on page 19 for details). If you prefer, use a black permanent marker and draw the mouth onto the crab as shown. Either way, be creative, and add some personality!

3. Brush a light coat of fabric glue on the wrong side of one of the bow ties. Be sure to brush the glue all the way to the edges to prevent fraying, practicing with scraps first. Place the bow tie onto the crab body, just below the mouth as shown. Clean excess glue off your fingers between applications. Repeat for each crab, using a different-colored bow tie for each to personalize them and help little players differentiate between them. Add details or embellish as desired—this will only make them cuter!

4. To make the eyes, place a thick dot of glue on the white felt circle, and adhere it onto the eyestalk. Place glue on the black felt pupil and adhere it onto the white of the eye. Repeat with all of the circles and eyestalks to make a total of eight eyes. Positioning of the eyes can really add quirkiness and personality to each crab, so don't worry about perfection. Let the glue dry completely before going on to the next step.

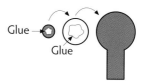

Glue — 〇   Glue

5. Assemble the crab by placing one crab body piece, with the mouth and bow tie facing up, on your work surface. Position the felt legs, pincers, and eyestalks wrong side up, facing inward. Be sure to leave at least a 2½" space between the crab legs; this will be the opening for turning. Place a plain crab body right side down on top. Pin to secure all parts in place. It's important not to sew any of the loose body parts into the seam.

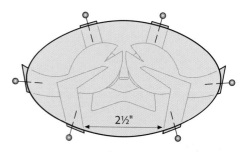

2½"

6. Using a ½" seam allowance, sew along the perimeter of the crab body. Leave a 2" opening at the bottom, between the two legs. Repeat for all four crabs.

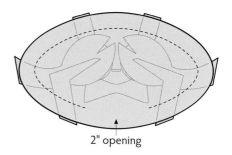

2" opening

7. Turn the crabs right side out and stuff them with the fiberfill through the opening at the bottom. For added weight, insert two tablespoons of pellets before adding stuffing. (Be sure to read "Safety Considerations" on page 11.) Machine or hand stitch the opening closed. If you densely stuff the crabs, you'll probably have to hand stitch them. However, there are only four, so hand stitching won't take long. Refer to "Ladder Stitch" on page 17 for detailed instructions. You can also use a blind stitch or slip stitch.

making the sand dollars

1. Mark the sand dollars for stitching as shown on the pattern. Stitch an ellipse around each of the four marked ovals and sew the "flower" design in the middle. In nature, each sand dollar is completely unique, so be spontaneous; you want them to be free-flowing and different. If you have a darning foot on your sewing machine for free-motion stitching, it works wonderfully here. Refer to "Free-Motion Stitching" on page 13 for additional details.

2. Cut out the center of the four outer ovals. I made a small slit first, and then gently stretched out each opening with my finger.

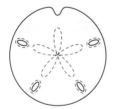

packaging your game

This game is an all-in-one project. Tuck your crabs and sand dollars into the pocket, roll up the mat, tie the roll, and you're ready to go!

Add a copy of the "How to Play Crab Crawl" game sheet on page 61, and you're done!

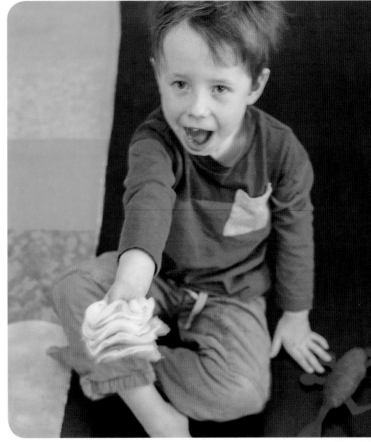

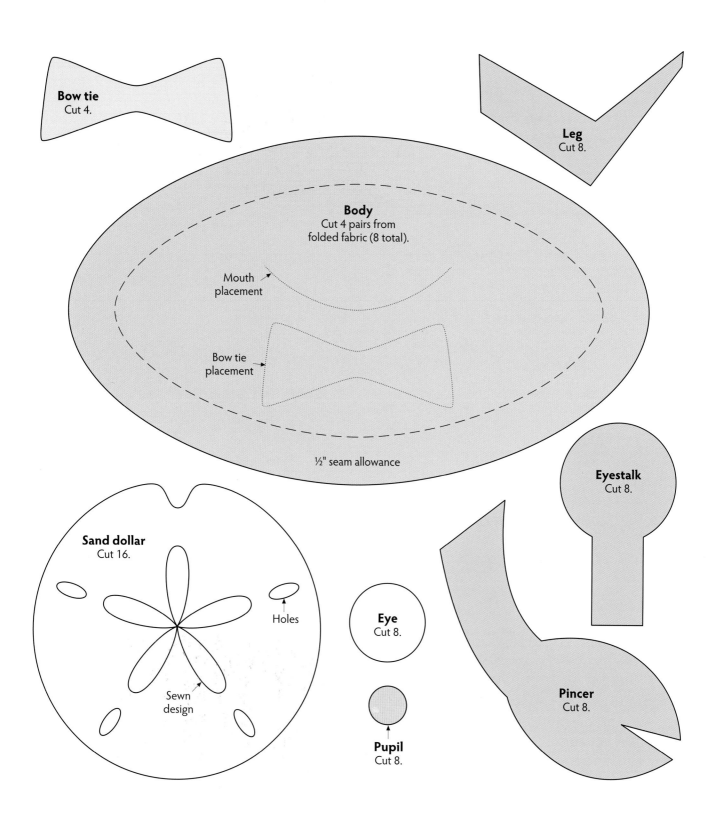

Bow tie
Cut 4.

Leg
Cut 8.

Body
Cut 4 pairs from
folded fabric (8 total).

Mouth
placement

Bow tie
placement

½" seam allowance

Eyestalk
Cut 8.

Sand dollar
Cut 16.

Holes

Sewn
design

Eye
Cut 8.

Pincer
Cut 8.

Pupil
Cut 8.

CRAB CRAWL ↲

Toddlers and Preschoolers

* **Crab Toss:** Place a laundry basket one to two feet away from the child; pile the crabs on the floor. On the count of three, ask the child to toss a crab into the laundry basket. Increase the challenge by increasing the distance of the basket.

* **Bitty Crab Crawl:** Lay out the mat, place the crabs randomly on the blue rectangles, and then stack the sand dollars next to the child. Tell the child that the crabs need to reach the beach before the storm! Together, pick a crab and count how many spaces it will take the crab to get to the beach. Ask the child to count out that number of sand dollars, and use those to pay the fisherman to help get the crab to shore. Take the sand dollars and let the child move the crab to the beach, counting each space as they move the crab. Repeat until all crabs have made it safely to the sand. This will help build early game-playing and math concepts.

School-Aged Kids

Crab Crawl (2 to 4 players)

Lay out the mat. Each player chooses one crab and one sand dollar. Put all of the extra sand dollars on the beach. The youngest player goes first. All players start at the blue end of the mat, far out at sea. The object of the game is to get your crab to the beach and collect sand dollars in order to win. The first player rolls the die and moves his or her crab that many spaces, toward the beach. If a crab lands on a space with a fishing net, the player must pay the fisherman one sand dollar in order to be released. The sand dollar is placed back on the beach. If players have no sand dollars, they lose their next turn as their crab takes extra time to escape from the net. To reach the beach, the player must roll the exact number needed in order to land on the beach. When a player's crab reaches the beach, the player gets a sand dollar and his or her crab returns to the ocean at the far end of the mat to begin the journey back to the beach again. Then the player rolls the die and continues on to his or her next turn. The first player to collect four sand dollars wins!

Crab Toss (2 to 4 players)

These crabs need to get to the beach—fast! Players take turns tossing all four crabs, starting far out at sea, at the blue end of the mat. For each crab that lands on the beach, the player gets a sand dollar, and the next round begins. When a player gets four sand dollars, the rest of the players toss to finish out the round, and the one who has the four sand dollars wins. If another player makes it to four in that round, the tying players each toss the four crabs again, one player at a time, to break the tie.

Snake Pit

This fast and furious game is amusing and full of excitement for all ages. Using coordination and speed, Snake Pit offers a dynamic game for kids to play in teams. These snakes also delight the little players and allow opportunities for simple games of tossing, counting, and matching. Get your scraps or fat quarters ready for these charming little reptiles.

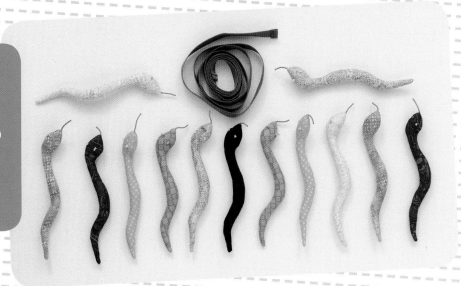

materials

Yardage is based on 42"-wide fabric.

¼ yard or 1 fat quarter *each* of 6 different-colored prints for snakes*

⅛ yard of black print for "black mamba" snake

¾ yard of pink parachute cord (size 95) or leftover vinyl for tongues

1 skein each of embroidery floss in 3 contrasting colors for snake eyes

3 yards of 1"- to 2"-wide nylon strapping for dividing line

12-ounce bag of fiberfill

Lightweight cardboard or template plastic

Candle or lighter for sealing parachute-cord ends

Optional sensory elements:**

26 jingle bells, ½"

1 sheet of cellophane (found in floral or gift-wrap departments at the grocery store)

I chose rainbow colors, but feel free to use more realistic or natural colors and prints as well. Just keep them different enough for color-matching preschool games if you plan to have little players.

**Be sure to read "Safety Considerations" on page 11 if you add these items.*

SNAKE EYES

I used embroidery floss to stitch French knot eyes because they're safe if chewed. Beads offer a creative alternative for older kids, but tiny seed beads are made of glass and present a choking hazard for little ones.

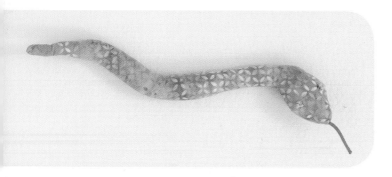

cutting

Make a template for the snake using the pattern on page 66. See the cutting guide below for cutting the snakes.

From *each* of the colored prints, cut:
2 snakes from folded fabric (2 and 2 reversed from each; 24 total)

From the black print, cut:
1 snake from folded fabric (1 and 1 reversed)

From the pink parachute cord, cut:
13 pieces, 1¾" long

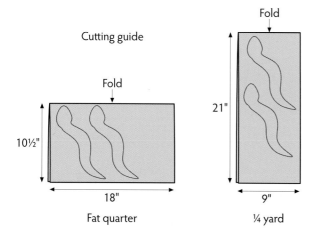

Cutting guide

Fold

10½"

18"

Fat quarter

Fold

21"

9"

¼ yard

making the snakes

1. Using the pattern as a guide, mark the eyes on the top piece of each pair of snakes. Double thread your needle with six strands of embroidery floss (12 strands total) and knot the end. Referring to "French Knot" on page 17,

bring the needle up through the first mark and make a French knot. Repeat at the second mark and tie off. Repeat to make eyes on each snake.

2. Referring to "Parts from Parachute Cord" on page 19, prepare 13 tongues for the snakes by sealing the ends of the 1¾" pieces of parachute cord.

3. Working with one pair of matching snake pieces, layer the top and bottom with right sides together. At the center of the snake's head, insert a pink tongue between the two pieces of fabric, centering it between the eyes as shown. Position the tongue so that 1" extends out beyond the seam when the snake is sewn and turned right side out. Baste or pin the tongue in place.

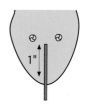

1"

4. Pin the two fabric layers together and sew around the snake body using a ¼" seam allowance. Leave a 1½" opening on the inside curve, as shown on the pattern. If you plan to insert bells, zigzag stitch around the perimeter, next to the straight stitching, for added strength. Stitch across the tongue again for extra durability. Trim the fabric at the point of the tail to reduce bulk.

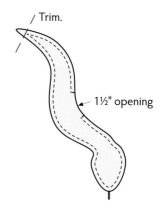

Trim.

1½" opening

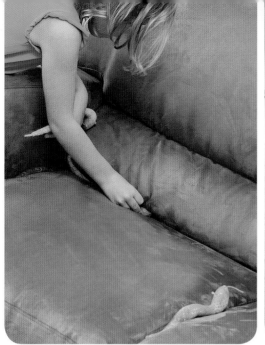

5. Turn the snake right side out. Use a chopstick, dull pencil, or other pointy object to gently poke inside to get the snake tails fully turned out (some fiberfill comes with a handy tool inside the bag). Be careful not to tear any stitching or fabric.

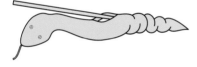

6. Repeat steps 3–5 for all of the snakes.

7. Stuff the snakes with fiberfill through the opening until they are firm throughout the head and body. If you are adding sensory elements such as bells and cellophane, stuff the tail with a small amount of fiberfill first, and then insert two or three bells. Stuff in some strips of cellophane, and then fill the rest with fiberfill.

8. Finish the snakes by hand sewing the side opening securely closed. For hand stitching details, refer to "Ladder Stitch" on page 17. (You can also use a blind stitch or slip stitch.) These snakes are easy to make, but it does take time to complete the hand sewing, so get cozy in a chair and enjoy the quiet time.

finishing the strap

Finish the ends of the strapping so that they will not fray. Fold each end down ½", and then fold another ½" to hide the cut edge. Topstitch ⅛" from the fold, backstitching at the beginning and end for extra security.

packaging your game

There are many fun options for storing this game. A tall rounded basket, similar to those used by snake charmers in the movies, might be a fun and easy solution for packing up this game. You can also use a picnic basket with a lid, a recycled wooden box, a spray-painted or decoupaged old tin, or a repurposed plastic storage container. I love to use the large canisters that pretzels and other snacks come in. If you prefer to sew something, the "Drawstring Bag" on page 104 or the "Classic Elastic Bag" on page 108 both work nicely.

Add a copy of the "How to Play Snake Pit" game sheet on page 67, and you're done!

¼" seam allowance

Leave open.

Snake

French knots

How to Play

SNAKE PIT

Toddlers and Preschoolers

The nylon strapping isn't needed for these games. Keep it out of reach of unsupervised children.

✳ **Tickle Snake:** Name a body part and tickle the child with the snake's tongue: "The tickle snake found your toes (nose, ears, neck, knees, hands)!" As children begin to learn where body parts are, give them a snake and ask them to "Show the tickle snake where your belly button (head, nose) is!"

✳ **Sister Snakes:** Place the snakes in a pile (remove the black mamba) and ask the child to pick out his or her favorite color. Then ask the child to find the snake's sister or look-alike. Name the color of the pair, set them aside, and then ask the child to select another one. Name the color and let the child find its match. As the child learns colors, start the game by asking for a specific colored snake and its match ("Can you find the green snake? Where is her sister?").

✳ **Snake Toss:** Place a laundry basket one to two feet from the child and the pile of snakes. On the count of three, ask the child to toss the snakes into the laundry basket, either randomly or by color. Increase the challenge by increasing the distance of the basket.

School-Aged Kids

Snake Pit (2+ players)

Lay the strapping along the center of the floor to divide the playing area. Form two teams and divide the snakes evenly between them, six snakes per team. Place the black mamba on the line in the middle. Teams stand on their side of the line. Get a one minute timer ready, or a short song cued up on your music player. The round begins when the timer/music starts, and ends when it stops. Players throw all of the snakes (including the black mamba) into the other team's playing area until the round is over. Count the snakes in each area: each snake equals one point, and the team with the *most* points ends up in the snake pit and loses. But players beware; the black mamba is worth two points!

Snake Hunt (2 to 4 players)

One player hides the snakes; the other players find them. Each snake is worth one point, matching pairs are worth three points, and the black mamba is worth four points. The player with the *most* points wins the hunt!

Snake Scavengers (2 to 4 players)

One player is the tour guide; the other players are adventurers. Each adventurer picks out one colored snake (not the black mamba) and holds onto it throughout the game. The tour guide takes the matching snakes and hides them, making secret notes on paper as needed. The tour guide gives one clue to each adventurer as to where his or her snake's mate is hidden (i.e., near where water runs, close to where you sleep, etc.). The first adventurer to find his or her snake's mate gets to be the tour guide once all other adventurers have completed the round. If a player requests another clue, other players have the option of getting another clue as well. If a player finds someone else's snake, don't tell or the other player will win!

Bug Hunt

Bug Hunt can turn any playing area into an exciting hide-and-seek adventure. Using the official bug tongs to collect their Jurassic-sized bugs, kids will enjoy playing this game again and again. The little ones will love the additional playing options that include sensory elements, counting, matching, and tossing. A new twist to a timeless game, this project can help you shrink your scrap pile and occupy the kids while you start your next Sew and Play project!

THE GAME CONSISTS OF:

- **6 pairs of matching 4" bugs**
- **1 creepy crawly spider**
- **2 pairs of tongs**
- **1 bug jar**

materials

Yardage is based on 42"-wide fabric.

⅛ yard or 1 fat eighth *each* of 6 different-colored prints for bug bodies*

⅛ yard of black solid for bug heads

4" x 11" piece of black premium felt or black solid for spider

1⅞ yards of black ribbon or rickrack for bug wings

7 yards of black leather or parachute cord for legs

1 skein of yellow embroidery floss for eyes

12-ounce bag of fiberfill

2 pairs of kitchen tongs (add 1 pair for each additional player over 3)

Lightweight cardboard or template plastic

Fabric-marking pen or pencil

Candle for sealing parachute-cord ends

Optional sensory elements (Read "Safety Considerations" on page 11):

   12 jingle bells, ¾"

   1 sheet of cellophane (found in floral or gift-wrap departments at the grocery store)

*Choose subtle prints in rainbow colors so that toddlers can name and match colors.

SCRAPPY BUGS

If you want to use up smaller scraps, choose one solid color for the bellies of all the bugs, and then use scraps for the tops. You'll only need a 6" x 8" piece of fabric for a matching bug pair, and an additional ½ yard of solid fabric for the bug bellies. You can use the same black fabric you use for the heads, or another dark color. A solid color that matches the print on top works well, too. Just be sure to keep it subtle. You don't want the fabric on the bellies to compete with the colors on the tops of the bugs, or make it confusing as to what color the bug is.

cutting

Make templates for the bug body, bug head, and spider using the patterns on page 72.

From *each* of the 6 different-colored prints, cut:
2 bug bodies from folded fabric (4 from each; 24 total)

From the black solid, cut:
12 bug heads

From the black felt, cut:
2 spiders

From the ribbon or rickrack, cut:
12 pieces, 5" long

From the leather or parachute cord, cut:*
80 legs, 3" long

*A rotary cutter makes it quick and easy to cut the legs.

making the bugs

Each layered pair of bug bodies will become one bug back and one bug belly. You'll make two bugs of each print.

1. On the right side of one bug body, sew a 5" ribbon or rickrack strip down the center. This will be the bug back. Repeat to make a total of 12 bug backs. Leave the bellies empty (pun intended).

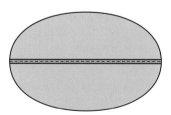

Make 12.

2. Place a black bug head, right side up, on top of each bug back. Align the curves of the bug head with the curve of the back. Pin in place and fold the straight, raw edge under

about ½". Topstitch along the folded edge to secure the head to the body.

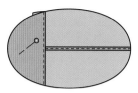

3. Mark the placement of the eyes on the black bug heads, using the pattern as a guide. Double thread your needle with six strands of yellow embroidery floss (12 strands total) and knot the end. Starting from the wrong side of the body fabric, bring the needle up through both layers of fabric at the first mark and make a French knot. Refer to "French Knot" on page 17 if necessary. Bring the needle up through the second mark, make another French knot, and tie off. Repeat to make eyes on each bug and the spider.

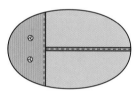

4. If you're using parachute cord for the bug legs, refer to "Parts from Parachute Cord" on page 19 and seal the ends of the legs to prevent fraying.

5. With the top of the bug right side up, place six bug legs around the back, three on each side as shown. When placing the legs, allow 2" to extend into the center of the bug back beyond the seam allowance. This will enable the bugs to have legs that are 2" long when finished, and will also leave a good amount secured into the seam. Leave at least 1⅜" of fabric between the back legs and the center back.

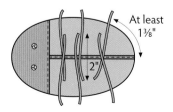

At least 1⅜"

2"

SECURE WIGGLY LEGS

It's helpful to tack the legs onto the fabric with a quick stitch at the edge before sewing the layers together. Cord can be slippery, and there are a lot of legs to monitor, so do this for all types of cords. Lift the presser foot as you approach each leg so that the leg doesn't move. Then lower the presser foot and stitch over the cord. Sewing works better than pinning and will keep the legs from shifting.

6. Place the matching belly piece on top of the back piece with right sides together. Pin the layers together and stitch carefully around the perimeter. Use a ½" seam allowance, and leave a 1¼" opening between the back legs.

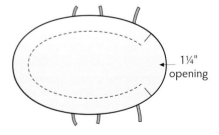

1¼"
opening

7. Repeat steps 5 and 6 for the spider using four legs on each side instead of three.

8. Turn each bug right side out, fill with stuffing until firm. If you're adding optional sensory elements, such as bells and cellophane, place these in the middle of the bug so soft stuffing surrounds them. Stitch the opening securely closed. You can fold raw edges in and topstitch with your sewing machine or hand stitch. If you stuff the bugs firmly, it will be easier to hand sew them closed. For hand stitching, refer to "Ladder Stitch" on page 17 for detailed instructions. You can also use a blind stitch or slip stitch.

packaging your game

This is a great opportunity to repurpose one of those large, plastic, lidded snack canisters into a bug jar! You can also purchase a clear plastic container, search the resale shops for a wire basket, or make a bag using a netting material. Refer to "Drawstring Bag" on page 104 or "Classic Elastic Bag" on page 108.

Add a copy of the "How to Play Bug Hunt" game sheet on page 73, and you're done!

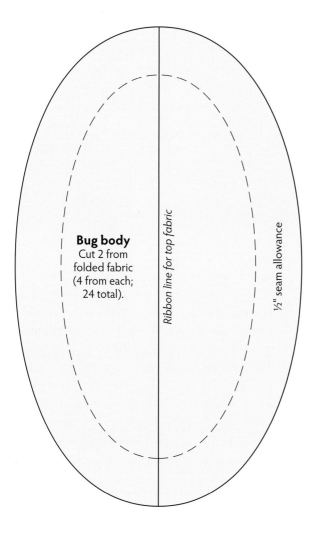

Bug body
Cut 2 from
folded fabric
(4 from each;
24 total).

Ribbon line for top fabric

½" seam allowance

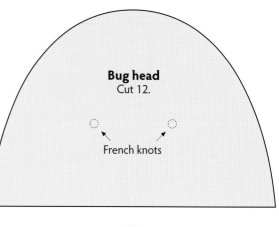

Bug head
Cut 12.

French knots

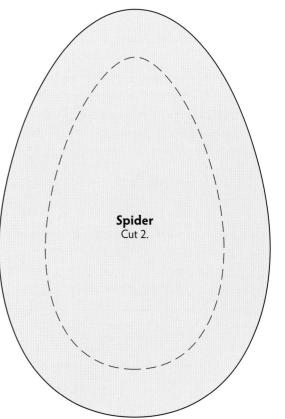

Spider
Cut 2.

Toddlers and Preschoolers

* **Color Bugs:** Let the child dump the bugs out of the jar. As the child puts them back into the container, name the colors of each bug. Ask the child to find the matching bug. As the child learns colors, ask him or her to put specific colored bugs into the jar (i.e., "Can you put the blue bug in the jar?").

* **Bitty Bug Toss:** Place a laundry basket one to two feet from the child. Pile the bugs on the floor. On the count of three, ask the child to toss the bugs into the laundry basket. As the child learns colors, prompt him or her to choose a specific color (i.e., "Throw the green bug into the basket!").

* **Bitty Bug Hunt:** In one room, "hide" all of the bugs at various levels, leaving them in view of the child. Ask the child to go on a bug hunt with you. Holding the bug jar, follow the child around as he or she finds the bugs, reaches to retrieve them, and then places them into the jar. Let children with good hand skills sit and practice picking up the bugs with the tongs. When they

master this task, let them play bug hunt like the big kids, using the tongs to retrieve them and deposit them in the bug jar.

School-Aged Kids

Bug Hunt (2 to 3 players)

You will need an additional pair of tongs for each additional player over 3. One player is the professor. This player takes the bug jar and hides all 12 bugs and the spider. The other players are the students; they go on a bug hunt with their tongs. When a student finds a bug, he or she must use the tongs to retrieve and call the color, and then place the bug in the jar. The professor keeps score and watches the students to make sure they aren't cheating! If a student does not use the tongs, he or she has to put the bug back for another student to grab.

Bugs are worth one point each, matching pairs are worth three points, and the spider is worth four points. The player with the most points wins and "graduates" to professor for the next round.

Bug Toss (2 to 4 players)

Place a laundry basket 10 feet away from the players and set the bug jar next to the players. Using only the tongs, players take turns retrieving a bug from the bug jar and throwing it into the basket. After each player throws all of the bugs and the spider, his or her points are tallied and the bugs are returned to the bug jar for the next player.

Bugs that land in the basket are worth one point each, matching pairs are worth three points, and the spider is worth four points. The first player to reach or score exactly 25 points wins! If a player goes over 25 points, they are out of the game. (Think of this as your bug jar tipping over and all the bugs crawling away!) Keep track of your points— players may need to intentionally miss the basket and await their next turn as their score gets close to 25.

The Castle AND THE Golden Eggs

The castle is close, but golden eggs are required to enter. Kids get to be the game pieces in this life-sized game of good fortune. Balancing as they walk around the stone path, kids are fully engaged in their quest for the castle. Younger players can easily follow along, as well as explore early-learning play with the golden eggs, and challenge their memory skills with the stones. Enjoy constructing this moderately easy project and watch those young imaginations soar.

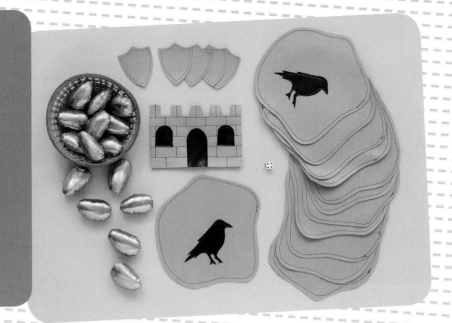

THE GAME CONSISTS OF:

- 10 stones (approximately 11" across)
- 15 golden eggs
- a 6" x 9" castle
- 5 shields
- 1 nest for eggs
- 1 die

materials

Yardage is based on 42"-wide cotton fabric and 54"-wide vinyl.

1⅞ yards of gray marine vinyl for stones, shields, and castle*

¼ yard of black marine vinyl for ravens and castle details*

½ yard of gold fabric for eggs

12-ounce bag of fiberfill

1 round basket, 8" to 12" diameter, for nest

1 die

Lightweight cardboard or template plastic

Machine upholstery needle and thread for sewing vinyl

Clear tape (with matte finish)

Fabric-marking pen or pencil

1-pound bag of plastic pellets (optional)**

Marine vinyl is available at most large fabric stores.

**Be sure to read "Safety Considerations" on page 11 if you include these.*

OTHER FABRIC OPTIONS

Vinyl is easy to clean, versatile for indoor and outdoor use, and does not fray. However, with a few additional steps and added materials, you could easily use cotton fabric instead. Add quilt batting (36" x 48") and fusible web (12" x 15") to your list and use the same patterns and fabric yardage as listed in the materials list. Then, refer to "Making the Islands" in "Treasure Island" on page 94 to make the stones. Use fusible web and black fabric for the ravens. Once the stones are assembled, stitch ½" from the edges to finish them. Simplify the castle by cutting a felt rectangle using stitching, black fabric, and fusible web to add details.

For the eggs, gold cotton is easy to sew. For a shiny, metallic eye-catching option, I used gold lamé with medium-weight fusible stabilizer. That will surely make for a happy goose!

cutting

Make templates for the stone, castle, castle details, shield, raven, and egg using the patterns on pages 79–81.

From the gray vinyl, cut:
10 stones from folded vinyl (20 total)*
1 castle from folded vinyl (2 total)
5 shields from the scraps

From the black vinyl, cut:
5 ravens
2 castle windows
1 castle door

From the gold fabric, cut:
15 eggs from folded fabric (30 total)

*If you find it difficult to cut the two layers of vinyl, trace the stone pattern onto a single layer of vinyl. Cut 10 stones using the pattern right side up; then cut 10 stones using the pattern right side down. This will give you 10 pairs that will match up as top and bottom pieces.

TIPS FOR SEWING VINYL

* *Use an upholstery needle and thread in your sewing machine.*

* *Increase the stitch length on your sewing machine to the longest setting to decrease excessive perforation of the vinyl.*

* *Prevent sticking by applying a strip of clear tape to the underside of the presser foot, trimming away any exposed edges. (Don't use the shiny tape; you want the translucent kind with the matte finish.) This will help the vinyl glide along easily as you sew.*

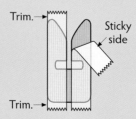

Trim.

Sticky side

Trim.

making the stones

1. Working in pairs, match the top and bottom pieces of gray vinyl with wrong sides together; you should have 10 pairs total.

2. Stitch a vinyl raven onto *the top piece of* each of five pairs of vinyl stones, stitching about ⅛" to ¼" from the edge of the raven. If you have experience with free-motion stitching, use a darning foot and stitch the raven in this manner. If not, sew slowly, raising and lowering the presser foot, pivoting as needed to stitch around the raven. Keep the stone pairs grouped together while attaching the ravens so they don't get mixed up.

3. With wrong sides together, stitch the stone pairs together with a ½" seam allowance around the entire perimeter. You should have a total of 10 stones, with the gray vinyl exposed on the top and the bottom. Five of the stones should have a raven on one side.

Make 5.   Make 5.

making the castle and shields

1. Layer the two castle pieces with wrong sides together, and stitch horizontal lines approximately 1" apart. (It's easiest to mark the horizontal lines first, and then start stitching near the center to avoid shifting of the two layers.) Complete the brick pattern by stitching vertical lines approximately 2" apart, staggering them from row to row, using the pattern as a guide.

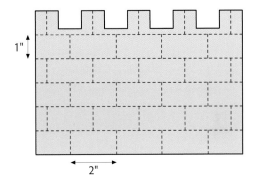

2. Using the same technique you used to attach the ravens, stitch the two windows and the door onto the top piece of the castle.

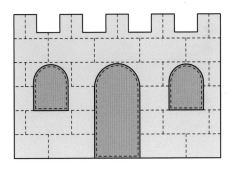

3. Stitch around the perimeter of each shield, about ⅛" from the edge. Feel free to get creative and add initials or a design in the center. Note that the shields consist of just one layer of vinyl.

making the eggs

1. Layer egg pairs with right sides together. Stitch around the perimeter of each egg, using a ½" seam allowance and leaving a 1" opening along the side near the top of the egg. Leave the opening along the straightest section toward the top of the egg to make sewing easier after stuffing.

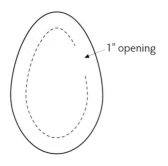

1" opening

2. Turn the eggs right side out and stuff with fiberfill. If you are including the optional pellets for some added weight, insert approximately one to two tablespoons of pellets before adding stuffing.

3. Hand or machine stitch the opening closed. If you stuff the eggs loosely, you can use your sewing machine. If you stuff the eggs firmly, it will be easier to hand sew them closed and they will look cleaner. For hand stitching, refer to "Ladder Stitch" on page 17 for detailed instructions. You can also use a blind stitch or slip stitch.

NEST IDEAS

* *If you crochet, make a nest from brown yarn—an upside-down hat is all you need!*

* *A basket from a secondhand shop or one tucked away in your attic would make an easy and eco-friendly nest.*

* *Use the fabric pottery techniques from the book* It's a Wrap *by Susan Breier (Martingale, 2006) to make a bowl-shaped nest. With clothesline, a variety of brown fabrics, and some textured yarns, your nest will be a work of art!*

packaging your game

Get really creative and decorate a lidded hatbox or a large, round popcorn tin using the castle theme. A drawstring bag would also be an easy way to keep the game pieces together (refer to "Drawstring Bag" on page 104).

Add a copy of the "How to Play the Castle and the Golden Eggs" game sheets on pages 82 and 83, and you're done!

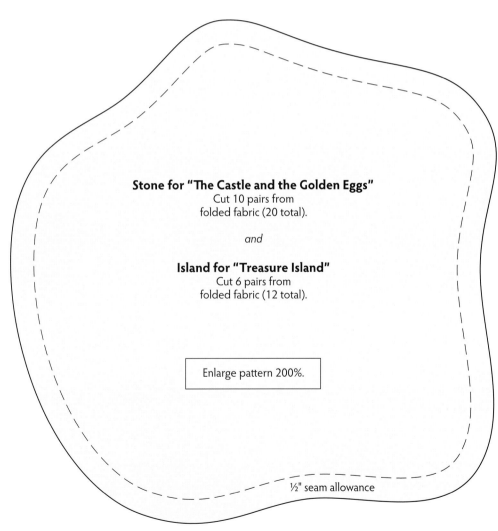

Stone for "The Castle and the Golden Eggs"
Cut 10 pairs from
folded fabric (20 total).

and

Island for "Treasure Island"
Cut 6 pairs from
folded fabric (12 total).

Enlarge pattern 200%.

½" seam allowance

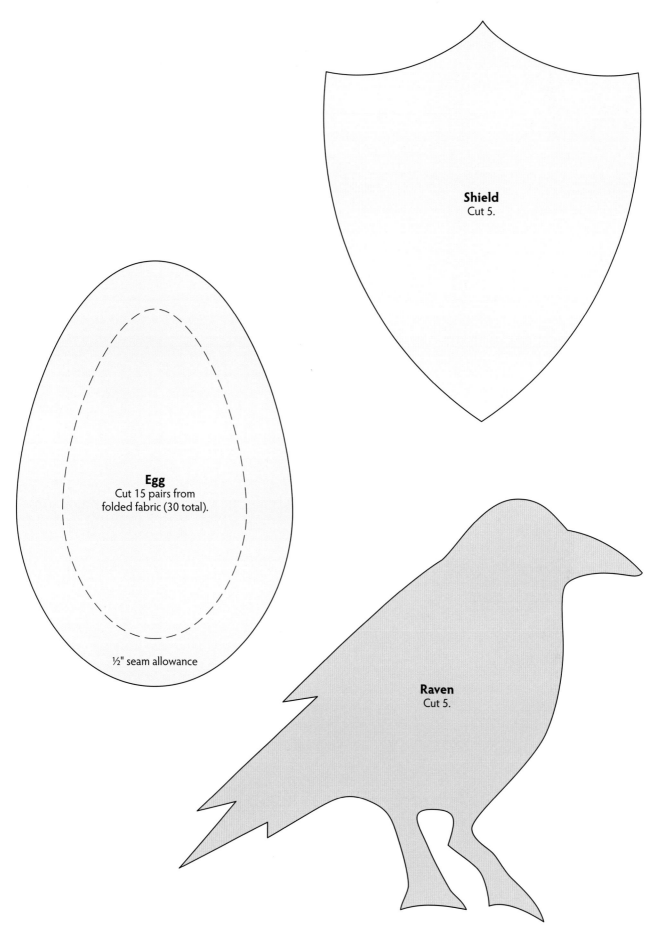

Shield
Cut 5.

Egg
Cut 15 pairs from
folded fabric (30 total).

½" seam allowance

Raven
Cut 5.

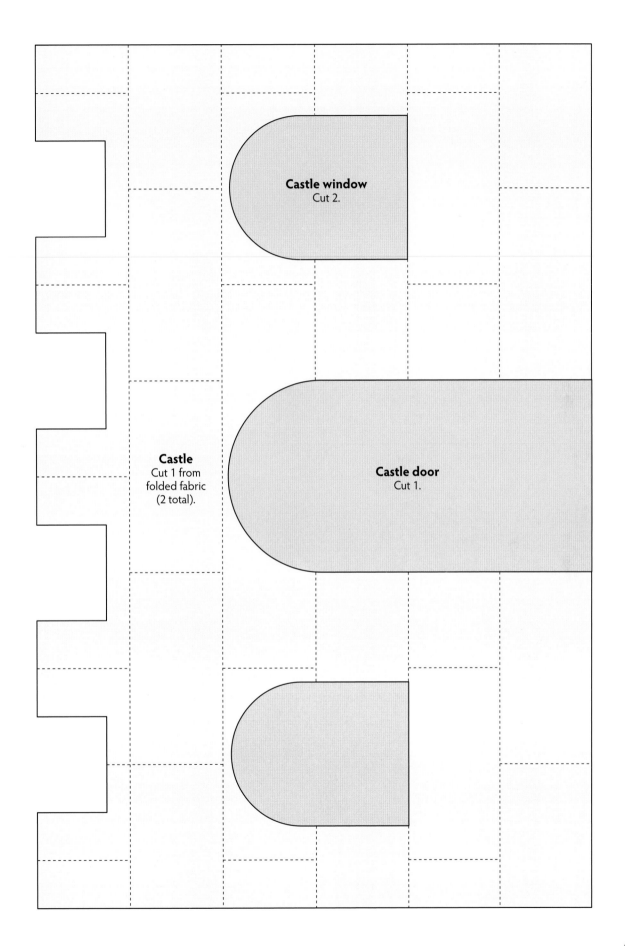

Castle window
Cut 2.

Castle
Cut 1 from
folded fabric
(2 total).

Castle door
Cut 1.

THE CASTLE AND ↩ THE GOLDEN EGGS

Toddlers and Preschoolers

These games are great ways to explore coordination, counting, and recollection.

* **Nest Egg:** Have the child count the eggs in the nest. Take away a few eggs, and have them count again. Add and remove eggs and let them count the pile of eggs each time. This helps children see the concept behind numbers and quantity.

* **Raven Hunt:** Select three stones, including one with a raven, and place them face up on the floor. Let the child look at them. Then flip them over, face down, hiding the raven. Ask the child where the raven (or black bird) went and see if he or she remembers. As the child plays, increase the challenge by adding more stones and ravens to the game.

* **Raven Magic:** Children love to play guessing games. Place three stones face up in front of you, including one with a raven. Now flip the stones over and shuffle the stones around, keeping them face down. See if the child can guess which one has the raven hiding under it.

* **Egg Hunt:** Place the stones on the floor in a path with the basket at one end. Now scatter the eggs around within reaching distance of the stones. Starting at the end of the path that is opposite the basket, have the child walk along the path and retrieve the eggs, bringing them to the basket.

THE CASTLE AND ↩
THE GOLDEN EGGS

School-Aged Kids

The Castle and the Golden Eggs (2+ players)

Set up the game by creating a circular path that connects completely and can be navigated by all players without having to step off the stones. Start the game with just one raven exposed. Place the castle outside the circle, by a stone that doesn't have a raven on it; this is the entry stone. Next to the castle, place the nest filled with the golden eggs. Each player will be a game piece. The player to roll the highest number goes first.

The first player rolls the die, keeping it in the center of the circle. Starting on the entry stone, the player counts and moves the number of stones rolled. Players must keep one foot on a stone at all times during the game. Each player takes a turn and then hands the die to the next player.

If a player lands on another player's stone, the player that rolled goes backwards to the stone that is not occupied. Once a player has made a full trip around and passes, or lands on, the entry stone, he or she gets a golden egg. Each trip around earns another golden egg for the player. If a player rolls a six and lands on or moves past the entry stone with this roll, he or she gets two golden eggs. But beware—ravens like shiny objects. Players who land on a stone with a raven must return one of their golden eggs to the nest.

During round 1, a player who has acquired five golden eggs must make one final, dangerous trip around the path back to the castle, rolling the die as before. If he or she succeeds with all five eggs still in hand, that player can enter the castle and be knighted, earning a shield. That ends round 1. Each time a player is knighted, the game starts over, and another stone with a raven is turned over, adding to the challenge of the game. As each new round starts, the number of eggs needed to enter the castle decreases. Refer to the table for each round.

Round	Ravens facing up	Eggs needed to enter castle for knighthood
1	1 raven	5 eggs
2	2 ravens	4 eggs
3	3 ravens	3 eggs
4	4 ravens	2 eggs
5	5 ravens	1 egg

At each new round, the player(s) not knighted rolls for the first move. The rounds are complete when all five ravens have been exposed and this final game is played to the end. The player that was knighted the most (has the most shields) after all five rounds wins the game.

Gone Fishin'

Gone Fishin' is a captivating and timeless game. It helps teach skill and patience, yet is accessible for many ages. The embellishments offer a delightful sensory experience for toddlers, as well as alternative playing options for older kids. Pull out your basket of ribbons, rickrack, and odds and ends to make this fabulous, fun, and fetching game!

THE GAME
CONSISTS OF:

- **40" x 45" pond mat**
- **6 matching pairs of fish (8" long)**
- **1 fishing pole (22" long)**

materials

Yardage is based on 42"-wide cotton fabric and 72"-wide premium felt.

2⅝ yards of green fabric for border, binding, and backing of pond mat

1 yard of blue fabric for pond

6 fat quarters (18" x 21") or ¼-yard cuts of assorted fabrics for fish

¼ yard of green felt or marine vinyl for lily pads

40" x 45" piece of quilt batting

16-ounce bag of fiberfill

2 skeins of embroidery floss for eyes

Assorted ribbons, yarns, and rickrack for embellishments

Rustproof safety pins for pin basting

2 yards of string for fishing line

24 zinc fender washers, ¼" x 1¼", for eyes

Large magnet with hole in center for fishing lure*

22" wooden dowel rod, ½" diameter, for fishing pole

Craft glue

Lightweight cardboard or template plastic

Fabric marking pen or pencil

1 or 2 wooden balls with ½"-diameter holes to cap fishing poles (optional)

Optional sensory elements:**

Jingle bells, ¾"

1 sheet of cellophane (found in floral or gift-wrap departments at the grocery store)

Hardware stores will have higher quality and stronger magnets than craft stores; find them near the bolts, screws, and fasteners.

**Be sure to read "Safety Considerations," on page 11 if you include these items.*

EMBELLISHMENTS

Each fish will require an assortment of three 4"- to 4½"-strips of ribbon, yarn, or rickrack for embellishment. Look for unique textures and visual appeal, such as fuzzy yarn or sparkly ribbons. Choose colors that match each corresponding fish to make colors easier for the little ones to identify.

cutting

Make templates for the fish and lily pad using the patterns on pages 89 and 90.

From the green fabric, cut:
1 rectangle, 40" x 45"
4 strips, 6" x 42"; crosscut into:
    2 strips, 6" x 34"
    2 strips, 6" x 40"
5 strips, 3" x 42"; crosscut *1 of the strips* into 2 strips, 3" x 11"

From the blue fabric, cut:
1 rectangle, 29" x 34"

From the green felt, cut:
6 lily pads

From *each* fat quarter, cut:
2 fish from folded fabric (4 from each; 24 total)

making the pond mat

1. With right sides together and using a ¼" seam allowance, sew the two green 6" x 34" strips to the blue 29" x 34" rectangle as shown. Press the seam allowances toward the green strips. Sew the green 6" x 40" strips to the right and left sides of the blue rectangle using a ¼" seam allowance. Press the seam allowances toward the green strips.

2. On a flat surface, place the green 40" x 45" backing rectangle wrong side up. Place the quilt batting on top and smooth it out. Place the pond with borders on top, right side up. Align the edges and pin together with safety pins.

3. Quilt the three layers together, starting from the center and working your way out. You can quilt in any design that is comfortable for you. I favor large swirls, since they allow me longer continuous stitching and, in this project, give the effect of water rippling from raindrops. Roll up the quilt neatly to fit the layers under the arm of the sewing machine.

4. Position and pin the lily pads onto the blue portion of the mat, spacing them evenly around the pond. Stitch them securely in the center with your sewing machine. I used free-motion stitching with a darning foot to stitch little flowers for added detail and decoration. Tacking only in the center gives the lily pads a three-dimensional appearance. You can wait to add the lily pads after the quilting is done if you prefer.

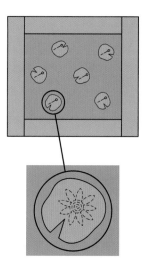

5. With right sides together and using a ¼" seam allowance, sew a green 3" x 11" strip to each of two of the green 3" x 42" binding strips along the short edge. The pieced strip should measure 3" x approximately 51".

6. Place the green 3" x 42" binding strips on the back of the mat, right sides together, aligning the raw edges with the mat's short edges. Pin and sew the strips to the back of the mat using a ½" seam allowance. Trim the short edges of the strips even strips even with the mat. Open the binding strips at the seam, exposing the right side of the fabric, and press the seam allowances toward the strips.

Place the 3" x 51" binding strips on the back of the mat, aligning the raw edges with the mat's long edges, and sew as you did before, using a ½" seam allowance with right sides together. Sew to the end of the mat, including the binding along the sides. Repeat with the opposite side. Trim any excess at each corner.

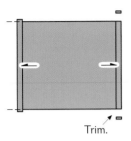 

Trim.   Trim.

7. Fold the binding over to the front of the mat, keeping it tight with the edge. Fold the raw edge of the binding under ½", and pin in place. Starting at least 6" from any corner, stitch ⅛" from the inner folded edge. At the corners, fold and tuck in a squared or mitered fashion, and then continue sewing until you have secured all four sides. This completes the mat.

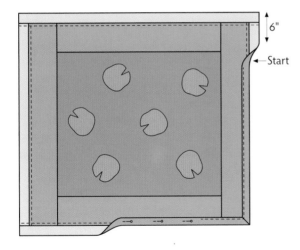

6"

Start

making the fish

1. Lay out one of the fish pieces. Place a zinc washer on the wrong side of the fabric, where the eye will go, and trace the inside and outside circles. Make sure that the washer is

centered and far enough away from the edge to allow for the ½" seam allowance when sewing the fish pairs together. This mark will guide you when you sew the washer to the fish. Repeat for all fish.

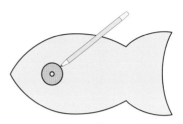

2. Place a washer onto the location you marked on the wrong side of the fabric. Double thread your needle with six strands of embroidery floss (12 strands total) and knot the end. To sew the washer onto the fish, start by inserting the needle into the center of the washer, at any point along the marked inner circle (to hide the knot on the inside). From the right side, bring the needle up through the fabric, at the outer edge, across from the knot. Insert the needle back down through the center of the washer, along the marked inner circle, next to the knot, and back up at the outer edge. Continue around the entire washer, in a fan-like pattern, spacing the outer stitches about ¼" apart, to fully secure the washer to the fabric. Take several small stitches and then knot the thread securely. This stitching will create the decorative embroidered eye on the outside while holding the washer in place on the inside.

Wrong side   Right side

3. Repeat step 2 for each fish (24 eyes total). The metal washer not only creates the magnetic capability of the fish, but it also adds some weight to increase the fun when tossing them.

4. Gather up your embellishments (ribbons, rickrack, yarns, etc.) and color coordinate them with the fish. Decorate *one* side of each fish with three to four strips of the embellishments. Lay them vertically, like stripes, on the right side of the fish body, staying at least an inch away from the eye. Sew them on securely with a straight, zigzag, or decorative stitch. These are ornamental and fun—be as creative as you like! Refer to the photo on page 89 for ideas.

5. With right sides together, pair the fish by color. Make sure that each fish has one embellished side and one plain side. The washers will be exposed on the wrong sides. Sew around the perimeter of the fish, using a ½" seam allowance and leaving the tail end open for stuffing. Note: Keep your seam allowance accurate, especially at the junction where the body and tail come together. This opening will be just big enough to allow you to squeeze the washers through when you turn the fish right side out.

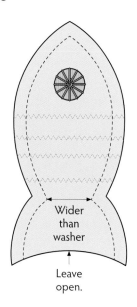

Wider than washer

Leave open.

6. Turn the fish right side out and stuff the body with fiberfill, leaving the tail empty to create a flat fin. If you are adding any sensory elements, be sure to insert fiberfill first, nestle the cellophane or bells in the middle, and then stuff the end with fiberfill.

7. Fold the open end of the tail under ½" and stitch ⅛" from the fold to close the opening.

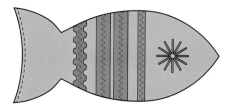

8. Create texture on the tail fin with stitching. You can get creative here, or sew a series of straight lines for a natural fish-fin look.

making the fishing pole

1. Using craft glue, attach an optional wooden ball to one or both ends of the dowel rod, and allow to dry.

2. Starting 3" from the end of the wooden dowel, tie the string around the dowel and knot it, leaving a tail approximately 1" long. Hold the string tail flush against the dowel, and wrap the other end of the string around the dowel, pulling the string through the loop as shown. Continue with this knotting until the string tail is completely covered. Add craft glue to the knots for added security.

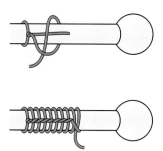

3. Thread the loose end of the string through the hole in the magnet. Allow about 40" for the finished length of the fishing line. Knot the string securely four to five times and glue the knots. Trim any excess string.

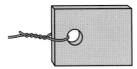

packaging your game

A drawstring bag made of netting material would be a great way to store this game (refer to "Drawstring Bag" on page 104). You can also save time and just buy a net laundry bag. A large tackle box or a bucket to keep the fish in would be a clever way to add to the theme. Get creative!

Add a copy of the "How to Play Gone Fishin'" game sheet on page 91, and you're done!

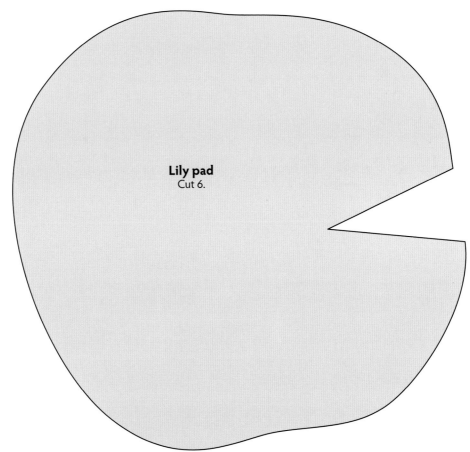

Lily pad
Cut 6.

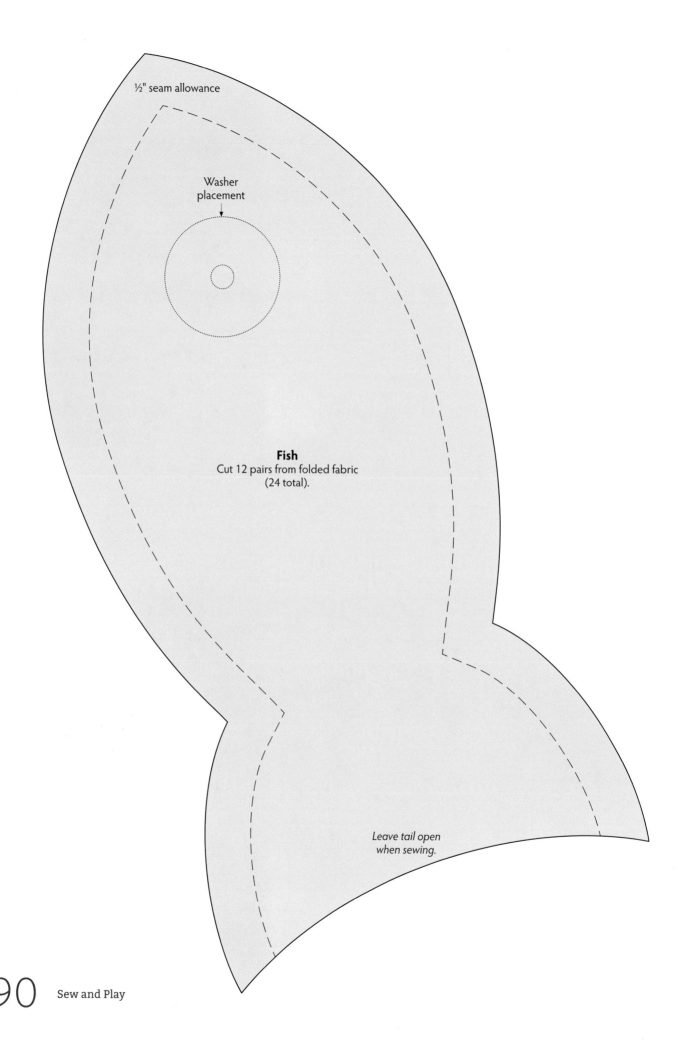

½" seam allowance

Washer placement

Fish
Cut 12 pairs from folded fabric
(24 total).

*Leave tail open
when sewing.*

How to Play
GONE FISHIN' ↵

Toddlers and Preschoolers

The fishing pole is intended for older children only. The long string from fishing line can get wrapped around wiggly little ones too easily—always supervise!

* **Fish Toss:** Place a laundry basket one to two feet from the child. Pile the fish on the floor. Ask the child to toss the fish into the laundry basket. As the child learns colors, prompt him or her to choose a specific color. Increase the challenge by increasing the distance of the basket.

* **Fish Friends:** Choose one fish and ask the child to find the matching fish. Continue with each color until all fish have found friends.

* **Fish Find:** In one room, "hide" all of the fish at various levels, leaving them in view of the child. Ask the child to go on a fishing trip with you. Hold the fishing net or bag, follow the child around to collect his or her catch.

School-Aged Kids

Gone Fishin' (2 to 4 players)

Divide the fish among the players. Players stand at any distance and toss the fish onto the mat in order to randomly set up the game. All fish must be completely on the mat. It's okay if they land on the green border. Any fish with their decorative sides up are considered "prize fish." Taking turns, each player uses the fishing pole to retrieve a fish. The object is to get the fish off the mat, and drop it by the player's feet. The magnet on the fishing pole will be attracted to the fish eyes. If a player makes contact with a fish, and lifts it completely off the ground, his or her turn has been taken, regardless of whether the fish falls or is caught. Plain fish legitimately caught are worth one point; prize fish are worth two points. When the fish have all been caught, the player with the most points wins!

Prize Fish Toss (2 to 4 players)

Divide the fish among all players. To determine the distance for tossing, players step back from the mat according to age (for example, four-year-olds take four steps back). Once in position, take turns throwing fish. Each player tosses all of his or her fish onto the mat. The object of the game is to get the fish back into the water. If fish land out of the water (on the border or off the mat), they cannot be tossed again.

Fish need to be more than halfway in the water to count. If a fish lands more than halfway on a lily pad, the player gets another chance to throw that fish. If a fish lands in the water with its decorative side up, it's a prize fish, worth the most points. Once a player has tossed all of his or her fish, he or she tallies the points and gathers the fish so the next player can throw. A fish in water equal two points; a prize fish in water equals three points. The first player to reach 10 points wins!

Treasure Island

Treasure Island is an adventure game with a hint of mystery in the search for hidden treasure. This game will capture the imaginations of kids while improving their coordination. Young players will love the element of surprise and enjoy the challenge of island hopping. Fun to make and fun to play, this game is worth the time and will create years of memories.

THE GAME CONSISTS OF:

- 4 sailboats
- 6 islands (approximately 11" wide)
- 25 gold coins
- 1 pirate flag

materials

Yardage is based on 42"-wide fabric.

1⅓ yards of light tan fabric for islands, hidden pockets, and pellet tubes

⅓ yard of brown fabric for boat decks and palm-tree trunks

⅛ yard of green print for palm trees

1 piece, 8" x 10", *each* of 4 assorted prints for boat hulls

1 piece, 3" x 10", *each* of black and white solids for boat windows and pirate flag

9" x 12" piece of yellow felt for gold coins

24" x 36" piece of quilt batting for islands

7" x 12" heavyweight stabilizer for boat sails and pirate-flag details*

12-ounce bag of fiberfill

1-pound bag of plastic pellets**

½ yard of 17"-wide fusible web***

I used Pellon brand Peltex 70 Ultra-Firm Sew-In Stabilizer.

**Read "Safety Considerations" on page 11.*

***If adding sewn details to the palm trees and windows (recommended), use sewable fusible web. Otherwise use no-sew fusible web.*

cutting

Make templates for the boat, sail, and flag using the patterns on pages 98 and 99, and the island using the pattern on page 79 (also used for stones in The Castle and the Golden Eggs).

From the light-tan fabric, cut:
6 islands from folded fabric (12 total)
6 rectangles, 4" x 4½"
4 rectangles, 3½" x 5"

From the batting, cut:
6 islands

From *each* of the 4 assorted prints, cut:
1 boat hull from folded fabric (2 of each; 8 total)

From the brown fabric, cut:
4 boat decks; cut each deck in half, down the center line, as indicated on the pattern

From the black fabric cut:
1 rectangle, 2" x 3"

From the heavyweight stabilizer, cut:
4 sails
2 bones
1 skull

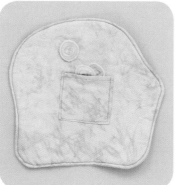

making the islands

1. Using the patterns on page 98 and referring to "Fusible Web" on page 14, trace six palm trunks and six palm leaves onto the paper side of the fusible web. Cut loosely around the patterns. Fuse the trunks to the wrong side of the brown fabric and the palm leaves to the wrong side of the green fabric. Cut out the trunks and palm leaves on the drawn lines.

2. Working in pairs, assemble one tree on the top of each pair of islands. Peel the paper backing off both the trunk and the palm leaves, and center the tree in the middle of the island. (Remember, you will lose ½" from all sides once the island pairs are sewn together.) Following the manufacturer's instructions, fuse the tree to the top of the island. Repeat for all six islands, using the original as a guide for uniform placement. Stitch around the perimeter of the tree and add a decorative crisscross pattern in the center if desired. Then add details to the palm leaves. Use a free-motion stitch for greatest flexibility. (Skip the stitching if you're using *no-sew* fusible web.)

Optional stitching

3. To make the hidden coin pocket, fold the short edge of the tan 4" x 4½" rectangle ¼" to the wrong side. Fold another ¼" to make a hem. Topstitch ⅛" from the inner folded edge. Make six coin pockets.

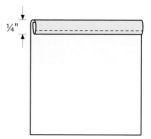

¼"

4. Fold the three raw edges of each coin pocket under ½" and press. Center a coin pocket right side up on the right side of an island piece *without a palm tree*. Pin, and sew it to the island around the three pressed sides. Repeat for all six islands.

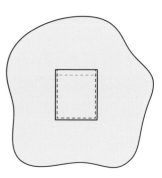

5. Place the island piece with the pocket right side up on your work surface. Place the island with the tree on top, right sides together and aligning the edges. Place the island-shaped quilt batting on top.

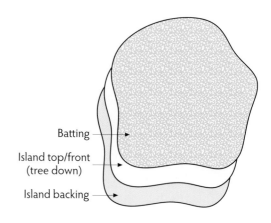

Batting

Island top/front (tree down)

Island backing

6. Sew around the perimeter of each island sandwich, using a ½" seam allowance and leaving a 3" opening along one edge.

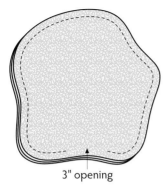

3" opening

7. Turn the islands right side out, fold under the open edges, and press. Topstitch along the opening, ¼" from the edge, and continue stitching around the island to finish. Repeat for all six islands.

Make 6.

making the boats

1. Using the patterns on page 98, trace 12 black windows and 12 white windows onto the paper side of the fusible web. Trace the circles in groups according to size. Cut loosely around the two groups of circles and fuse the 12 larger windows to the wrong side of the white fabric and the 12 smaller windows to the wrong side of the black fabric. Cut out the circles on the drawn lines.

2. Peel the paper backing off the circles. With the boat-hull fabric right side up, position three of each white and black window circles as shown, fusible side down onto *one* boat hull. Center them carefully, allowing space

for the ½" seam allowance when sewing the boat-hull pairs together. Fuse the windows to the boat hull and add stitching details if you are using the sewable fusible web. Repeat for four boat hulls. Boats will have windows on only one side.

Make 4.

3. Lay one boat-deck piece, right side up, and place an interfacing sail on top, aligning the shortest side with the center of the boat deck as shown. Place the other side of the boat deck on top with the right side down. Using a ½" seam allowance, sew along the straight edge to attach the sail and assemble the deck. Make four.

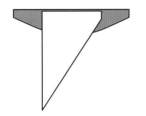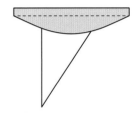

4. Pin two matching boat hulls right sides together, aligning the curved edges. Mark where the opening will be, using the pattern as a guide. Sew along the curved edge, leaving an opening as shown.

Leave open.

5. Insert the sail, with attached boat deck, into the body of the boat, keeping the right sides in. This may be a little tricky, but just take your time and use pins. The sail should nestle perfectly into the opening that you left on the bottom of the boat. If it fits awkwardly, try turning the sail around to face the other direction. With the right sides of the boat hull and the boat deck together, pin carefully around the entire perimeter, making sure that the raw edges are aligned and that the seams match (remember, they don't have to be perfect). Using a ½" seam allowance, slowly sew the deck to the boat hull. Check your stitching; rip out and resew if there are pleats or puckers you can't live with. Use the opening where the sail is to gently pull the boat right side out.

6. To make the weighted tube, fold the tan 3½" x 5" rectangle in half along the width, and sew the bottom and side edge using a ½" seam allowance. This will create a little tube to put the weighted pellets into. Turn right side out.

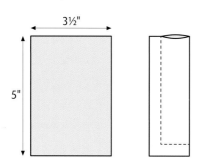

7. Fill the tube with pellets, leaving 2" at the top. Fold the opening over ½", and then another ½" so the raw edge is tucked in. Sew the tube closed. Repeat to make four. This little tube will weigh the boats down at the bottom, making them easier to land on the island without capsizing.

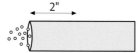

8. Through the opening, stuff the boats with fiberfill, and then insert the weighted tube at the bottom.

9. Hand sew the opening closed, repeating for all four boats. For detailed instructions on hand stitching, refer to "Ladder Stitch" on page 17. You can also sew the opening with a blind stitch or slip stitch.

making the coins and pirate flag

1. Make a template for the coins using the coin pattern on page 98. Trace 25 coins onto the yellow felt.

2. Using a free-motion stitch, sew swirls or spirals onto each coin while the felt is still in one piece. I used gold thread to make the swirls. Cut out the coins. Of course, you can skip the sewing if you prefer and cut the coins out without stitching.

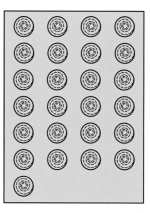

3. Sew a straight stitch around the perimeter of the black 2" x 3" flag rectangle about ⅛" from the edges. This will allow for some fraying along the edges to add authenticity and create a tattered flag. Lay the bones crisscross at the bottom of the flag, leaving room for the skull just above. Sew the bones to the flag with a jagged, free-motion or zigzag stitch through each. Black thread adds character to the bones. Position the skull just above the intersection of the bones, and use a free-motion stitch to detail eye and nose holes onto the skull, and then stitch the mouth. If all of the tiny pieces are two difficult to manage, just use the two crossbones centered on your flag. If you are more comfortable using a permanent marker to draw skull details, then just stitch the perimeter and draw on details, allowing time for the marker to dry before handling it.

packaging your game

To store this game, how about making a drawstring bag from nautical- or pirate-themed fabric? (Refer to "Drawstring Bag" on page 104.) Or, decorate a box to look like a treasure chest and store all of your game pieces inside!

Add a copy of the "How to Play Treasure Island" game sheets on pages 100–101, and you're done!

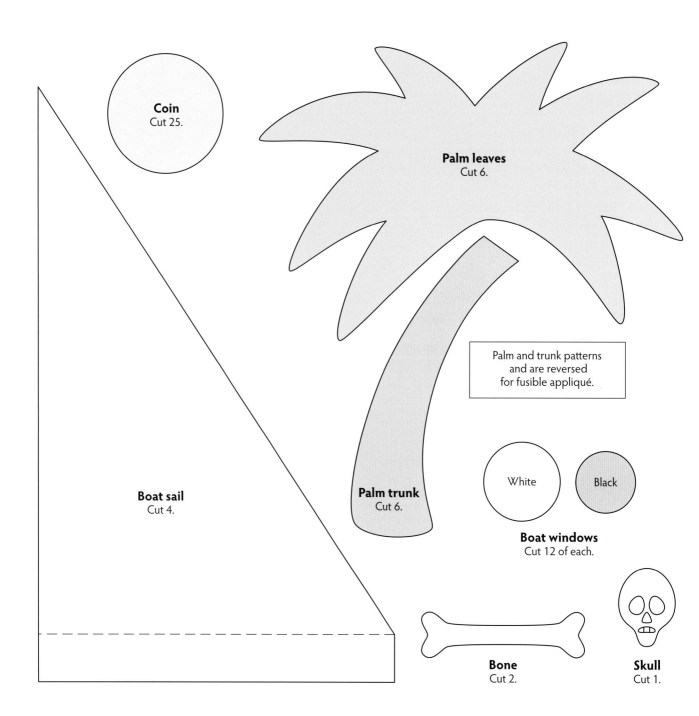

Coin
Cut 25.

Palm leaves
Cut 6.

Palm and trunk patterns
and are reversed
for fusible appliqué.

Boat sail
Cut 4.

Palm trunk
Cut 6.

White

Black

Boat windows
Cut 12 of each.

Bone
Cut 2.

Skull
Cut 1.

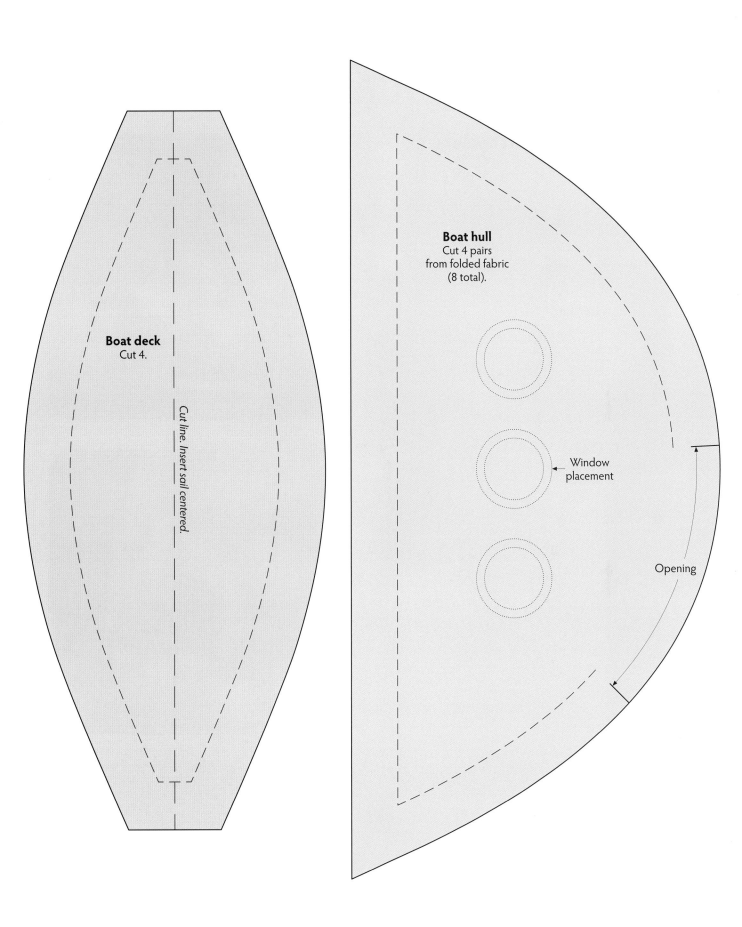

Boat deck
Cut 4.

Cut line. Insert sail centered.

Boat hull
Cut 4 pairs
from folded fabric
(8 total).

Window
placement

Opening

TREASURE ISLAND ↩

Toddlers and Preschoolers

* **Boat Collector:** Lay the islands out in a path, close enough together for the child to walk from one to the next. Scatter the boats on either side of this path and have the child reach to collect the boats, staying on the islands at all times. Increase the challenge by increasing the distance of the islands and the boats.

* **Buried Treasure:** Use just three of the islands for this game. Stash 10 or more coins into the three pockets, in varying amounts between the islands. Lay out the three islands and have the child choose one, pick it up, and count their coins. (Help as needed.) Pick another island and count the coins. When the child collects 10 coins he or she can buy a boat!

* **Catch the Pirate:** Hide the pirate flag in one of three islands, shuffle and lay them out with the palm-tree sides up. Ask the child to guess which island has pirates on it. When he or she selects one, turn it over and check the pocket. If it contains the pirate flag, hooray! Hide it again, shuffle, and repeat.

* **Boat Toss:** Place a laundry basket one to two feet from the child. Pile the boats on the floor. On the count of three, ask the child to toss a boat into the laundry basket. Increase the challenge by increasing the distance of the basket. Islands toss like Frisbees and can be fun, too!

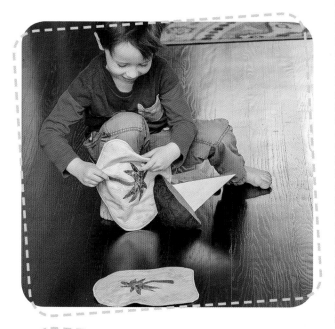

How to Play
TREASURE ISLAND

School-Aged Kids

Treasure Island (2 to 4 players)

Setup: One player hides the 25 coins in the island pockets, varying the amounts between islands for greater surprise. Another player shuffles the islands and places them on the floor with palm trees up, spacing them at least one foot apart from each other.

Players each choose a boat and take steps back according to age (for example, five-year-olds take five steps back). Let the youngest player toss first. If a boat lands partially or completely on an island, that player collects the treasure of coins in that island's pocket and returns the island to its place. The next player tosses. The object of the game is for one player to get 12 coins in order to win. If all islands become stripped of their treasure before this happens, the player with the most coins wins. Increase the challenge by increasing the distance that players stand from the islands when tossing.

Variation: Stash the pirate flag in one of the islands. The player who lands on that island must forfeit all of his or her coins and scatter them among the tops of the islands, distributing them as he or she chooses.

Island Empire (2 to 4 players)

Setup: One player hides the 25 coins in the pockets of five islands, varying the amount of coins between islands. In the sixth island, the player hides the pirate flag. Another player shuffles the islands, and places them on the floor with the palm trees up, spacing them at least one foot apart from each other.

Players each choose a boat and take steps back according to age (for example, five-year-olds take five steps back). The youngest player tosses first.

If a boat lands partially or completely on an island, that player collects the treasure of coins in that island's pocket and returns the island to its place. The next player tosses. The object of the game is to buy the islands and build an island empire. Once a player has five coins, he or she can buy an island on his or her next turn(s), if the boat lands on it. The player keeps the island, taking it out of the game, and then places five coins on top of the other islands, in any distribution. These coins will then be given as part of the treasure to the next player who lands on the islands.

If a player lands on an island with the hidden pirate flag, then, "Hark, pirates have stolen yer bounty!" The player must forfeit all coins and place them on top of the islands being played, to be acquired by any player that lands on those islands. The pirate flag is removed. This player doesn't lose any purchased islands. Once all of the islands have been bought, the player with the largest empire wins. Now play again!

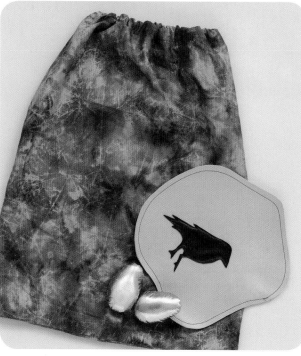

Game Accessories

In this section, you'll find instructions for all of the suggested game bags, as well as instructions on how to simplify some elements of the projects.

game storage bags

A variety of fabric bags are mentioned in the projects. They can be embellished as much as you like, or kept simple and sweet! If you have the time and are feeling crafty, why not assemble your project scraps into a clever patchwork drawstring bag to store the game?

Calculating Bag Materials

You will need to join two panels of the same size in order to construct a bag. Since each project is different, the size of each bag will vary as well. Here are the steps for determining the measurements of the two panels.

1. Fold or roll your completed project up loosely, game pieces and all. Measure the circumference of the bundle. This measurement will be used to calculate the *width* of the two panels.

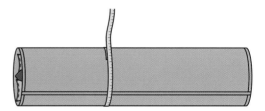

2. Measure the bundle from top to bottom; perpendicular to the measurement taken in step 1. Be sure to start at the base, and then go up, over, and back down so the full thickness is accounted for. This measurement will be used to calculate the length of your panels.

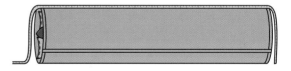

3. Add 8" to *each* measurement. This 8" is the extra fabric to allow for the sleeve/hem at the top, seam allowance, as well as extra room on the inside of the bag to make repacking the game easy.

4. Divide the width measurement in half to transform the total width measurement into the two panels that you need.

Let's say my project bundle is 20" in circumference and 12" in length. We'll use those numbers in the formulas below.

Width: Width + 8"; divide by 2

Example: 20" + 8" = 28"; divide by 2 = 14"
The width of the two panels will be 14" each.

Length (how tall the bag will be): Length + 8"

Example: 12" + 8" = 20"
The length of the two panels will be 20".

Length of cording for drawstring bag:
Circumference + 16"

Example: 20" + 16" = 36"
The length of cording needed is 36".

Length of elastic for either elastic bag:
Width of panel + 1"

Example: 14" + 1" = 15"
The length of ¼"-wide elastic needed is 15".

Note: If the elastic seems too loose as you feed it through the sleeve and cinch up the bag, feel free to shorten it by overlapping the tails more than 1". You want your hand and all of the game items to fit through the top easily, yet you don't want the elastic so loose that things can fall out easily.

Length of ribbon for elastic draw-bag casing:
Width of panel + 2"

Example: 14" x 2 = 28"
The length of ribbon needed is 28".

Note: If you are working with fabric that is stretchy, add 5" to 6" of extra ribbon. This will ensure that you don't run short of ribbon as you sew it around the bag. Just trim as you approach the end and fold the raw edge under as directed.

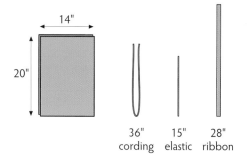

Drawstring Bag

This bag is a great, easy way to store any of these games. It's simple to construct and can be decorated in a multitude of ways. You can add letters cut from fabric and fusible web to spell the game's name. Or use the embroidery function on your sewing machine to add some images that match the game's theme. Just be sure to add these details to the *front* panel before you begin assembling the bag, following the instructions below.

You'll need:*
Fabric (two panels)
Parachute cording
1 cord stop, large size

Refer to "Calculating Bag Materials" on page 103 for panel and cord dimensions.

1. Fold top edge (the width) of one panel ¼" to the wrong side. Fold another ¼" to make a hem. Pin and topstitch ¼" from the inner folded edge. Repeat with the second panel.

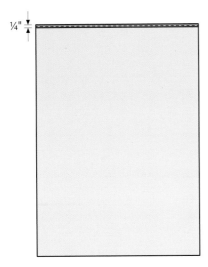

¼"

2. Layer the two fabric panels, right sides together, with the hemmed edges at the top. Measure and mark 3" down from the top corners. Beginning at the 3" mark, sew all three sides using a ½" seam allowance. Backstitch at the beginning to secure the seam. Stop stitching at the opposite 3" mark and secure with a locking stitch or backstitch.

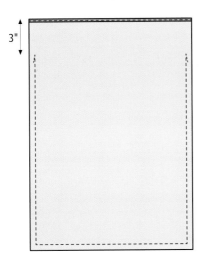

3"

3. Fold the raw edges of one of the open seams ¼" to the wrong sides. Sew down one folded edge and up the other, forming a long, squared V as shown. Repeat on the other side.

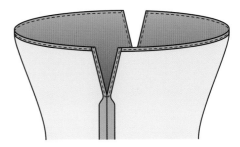

4. Fold the top edge of the bag 1½" to the wrong side and sew along the hemmed edge to create the sleeve for the drawstring. Repeat on both sides of the bag.

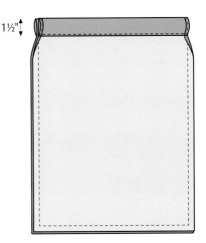

1½"

5. Referring to "Parts from Parachute Cord" on page 19, seal the ends of the parachute cord to prevent fraying.

6. Turn the bag right side out, and thread the cord through both sleeves. Use a safety pin to help feed it through.

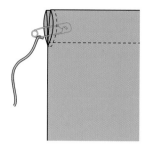

7. Thread both ends of the cord through the cord lock by depressing the spring-loaded button and revealing the hole. It helps to thread both ends through the hole together. Knot the ends together, securing the cord lock onto the cord.

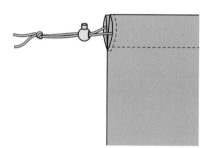

Elastic Draw Bag

This bag is designed perfectly for use as a "Draw Bag" so when little players are drawing from it, they cannot fall prey to temptation and peek! Unlike the classic elastic bag, it has a nifty "neck" of fabric at the top for little hands to hold onto while drawing.

To determine how much ribbon you'll need, refer to "Length of Ribbon for Elastic Draw-Bag Casing" on page 104. Ribbon that is ⅞" to 1" wide works well if you are using the recommended ¼" elastic.

1. Layer the two fabric panels with right sides together. Pin and sew along two sides and the bottom using a ½" seam allowance. Leave the top open.

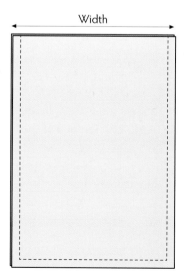

Width

2. Fold the top edge ¼" to the wrong side. Fold another ¼" to make a hem. Pin and topstitch ⅛" from the inner folded edge.

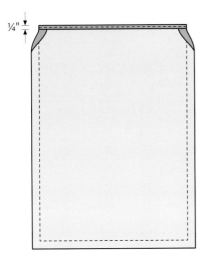

3. Turn the bag right side out. Measure 2" down from this hemmed edge and mark a line that is parallel with the top of the bag.

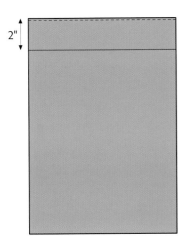

4. To make the casing for the elastic, start from a center point on either side of the bag, and lay your ribbon with its top edge along the marked line. Fold the raw end of the ribbon under. Following the line, pin the ribbon around the circumference of the bag, meeting up with the beginning of the ribbon. Complete by folding the remaining raw end of the ribbon under, lining it up with the beginning

of the ribbon. Trim the ribbon to the length needed. If you're working with stretchy fabric, however, wait until you've sewn most of the ribbon in place before trimming.

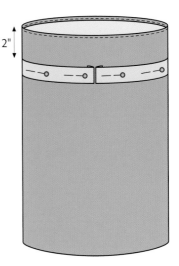

5. Stitch the top edge of the ribbon to the bag and then stitch the bottom edge, leaving the folded ends open for inserting the elastic.

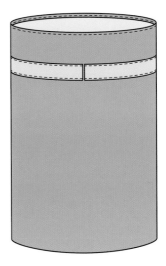

6. Using a safety pin attached to the end, feed the elastic through the opening in the casing. Hold the loose end tightly as you feed the other end all the way around the bag.

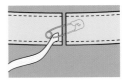

7. Overlap the ends of the elastic by 1" and sew them together securely. Stitch over this area multiple times for increased durability.

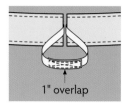

1" overlap

8. Let the elastic contract and hide inside the ribbon casing.

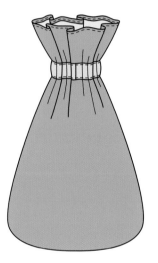

Classic Elastic Bag

This is a classic, incredibly easy-to-construct, elastic bag. Versatile and fast, this bag can be used to store any of the games in this book. Make an extra one to hold all of your scraps!

1. Layer the two fabric panels with right sides together. Pin and sew along two sides and the bottom using a ½" seam allowance. Leave the top open.

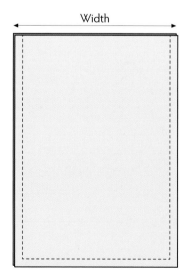

Width

2. Fold the top edge ¼" to the wrong side. Fold another ¼" to make a hem. Pin and topstitch ⅛" from the inner folded edge. (You can save time and simply press these folds in place. They will be sewn in the next step.)

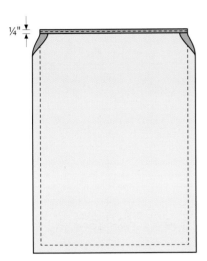

3. Fold the hemmed edge 1½" to the wrong side and, starting in the center of one of the panels, sew along the bottom fold to create a casing for the elastic. Stitch around the bag, leaving a 1" opening at your starting point. This is where you will insert the elastic.

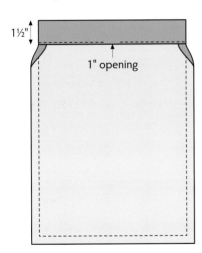

4. Insert the elastic into the casing using a safety pin.

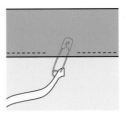

5. Overlap the ends of the elastic by 1" and sew them together securely. Stitch over this area multiple times for increased durability.

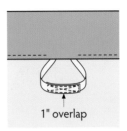

6. Finish the bag by stitching the 1" opening of the casing closed.

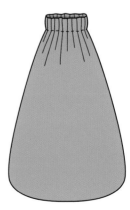

foundations

Some of the games require the construction of a foundation or mat of some sort. While I love the look and feel of the quilted mats, it's important to remember that kids will have just as much fun with any variation, since changing the look doesn't change the game at all. Therefore, I'm offering several options to choose from based on your time, skill level, and budget.

Minimal Time, Skill, and Cost

If you choose to go with this easiest option, you'll only need to purchase the fabric required for the top piece of the foundation. You may omit the backing, batting, and binding.

1. Cut the top piece as instructed, and place it right side down. Starting with any side, fold the edge ½" to the wrong side. Fold another ½", hiding the raw edge. Pin and topstitch ⅛" from the inner folded edge. This will essentially look similar to the hem you see on clothing.

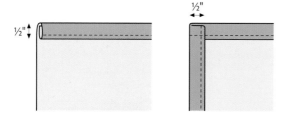

2. Repeat step 1 with each of the remaining three sides. When you encounter the corners, you may fold them down to keep them square, as shown, or tuck the corner in at an angle to create a mitered corner. I prefer the square, and it's the easier method.

3. Press the completed foundation and continue with instructions as your project directs.

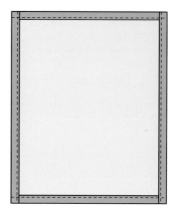

Moderate Skill

Use this option if you don't want to add binding strips as directed in the project. You will need the fabric required for the top, backing, and batting. Omit any fabric required to make strips for the binding.

1. Cut the top, backing, and batting as instructed. They should all be the same size.

2. Place the backing fabric on a flat surface, right side up. Place the top fabric right side down, and then add the batting on top. Smooth out the layers and pin together.

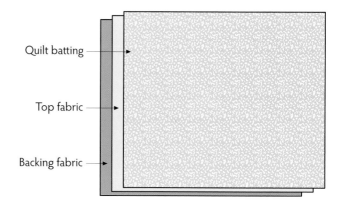

3. Sew the three layers together along the perimeter using a ½" seam allowance. Leave a 6" opening in the middle of one side. Trim the corners to reduce bulk.

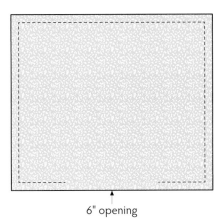

6" opening

4. Turn the assembled fabrics right side out through the opening, pushing corners out fully.

5. Topstitch the opening closed, stitching ¼" from the edge. You may continue stitching around the entire perimeter for added detail if you desire. Press the completed foundation and continue with instructions as your project directs.

ACKNOWLEDGMENTS

For my grandmother Frances, who played for hours with us, and inspired me to pick up a needle and thread. For my parents, Denny and Verena, who never give up on me. For my brother and best friend Deric, who has been my biggest fan, and believed all things possible. For little Devin, who has blessed this world again. For Nick and Tessa, my first loves, who gave me the original inspiration for this book. For my children, who make my heart smile every day. And for my husband, Ken, with his heart of gold and unconditional support, who tolerated months of household disarray, fabric hoarding, and prepackaged meals. My deepest gratitude to you all.